# Igniting Real Change for Multilingual Learners

In schools across the country, educators are serving more and more multilingual students and families. This book equips you with the considerations, tools, and resources you need as you fight for equity and advocate for those you serve.

Author Carly Spina unpacks a variety of approaches and lenses, including multi-tiered systems of support (MTSS) structures, family engagement, centering student experiences, and nurturing and cultivating a multilingual mindset throughout school classrooms and communities. Each chapter provides practical tools, tips, and vignettes to help you go beyond the "why" to take action. Throughout the book, you will be called to Question, Equip, and Act!

As you work through the book, you'll be inspired to move your systems forward on your equity journey for multilingual students. Get ready to Ignite Real Change!

**Carly Spina** has almost two decades of experience in multilingual education, including her service as an EL teacher, a third-grade bilingual classroom teacher, and a district-wide multilingual instructional coach. She is currently a multilingual education specialist at the Illinois Resource Center. Her first book, *Moving Beyond for Multilingual Learners*, was a 2023 Equity in Excellence Award Winner. She is on most social media platforms, and you can find her at @MrsSpinasClass.

# Equity and Social Justice in Education Series
Paul C. Gorski, Series Editor

Routledge's Equity and Social Justice in Education series is a publishing home for books that apply critical and transformative equity and social justice theories to the work of on-the-ground educators. Books in the series describe meaningful solutions to the racism, white supremacy, economic injustice, sexism, heterosexism, transphobia, ableism, neoliberalism, and other oppressive conditions that pervade schools and school districts.

**Becoming an Everyday Changemaker**
Healing and Justice at School
*Alex Shevrin Venet*

**Embracing the Exceptions**
Meeting the Needs of Neurodivergent
Students of Color
*JPB Gerald*

**Identity-Conscious Practice in Action**
Shaping Equitable Schools and Classrooms
*Liza Talusan*

**Social Studies for a Better World, Second Edition**
An Anti-Oppressive Approach for
Elementary Educators
*Noreen Naseem Rodríguez and Katy Swalwell*

**Teaching Storytelling in Classrooms and Communities**
Amplifying Student Voices and Inspiring Social Change
*Maru Gonzalez, Michael Kokozos, and Christy Byrd*

**Igniting Real Change for Multilingual Learners**
Equity and Advocacy in Action
*Carly Spina*

# Igniting Real Change for Multilingual Learners
## Equity and Advocacy in Action

Carly Spina

Routledge
Taylor & Francis Group
NEW YORK AND LONDON

Designed cover image: Getty Images

First published 2025
by Routledge
605 Third Avenue, New York, NY 10158

and by Routledge
4 Park Square, Milton Park, Abingdon, Oxon OX14 4RN

*Routledge is an imprint of the Taylor & Francis Group, an informa business*

© 2025 Carly Spina

The right of Carly Spina to be identified as author of this work has been asserted in accordance with sections 77 and 78 of the Copyright, Designs and Patents Act 1988.

All rights reserved. No part of this book may be reprinted or reproduced or utilised in any form or by any electronic, mechanical, or other means, now known or hereafter invented, including photocopying and recording, or in any information storage or retrieval system, without permission in writing from the publishers.

*Trademark notice*: Product or corporate names may be trademarks or registered trademarks, and are used only for identification and explanation without intent to infringe.

ISBN: 978-1-032-82336-2 (pbk)
ISBN: 978-1-003-51438-1 (ebk)

DOI: 10.4324/9781003514381

Typeset in Palatino
by Apex CoVantage, LLC

To my husband Eric—Thank you for always believing in me and cheering me on in all my wildest dreams. I'm so thankful for you.

To my TJ and Chloe—I love you both beyond this world, and I am endlessly proud of the amazing human beings you are. You are the most important people in my life.

To my parents, Jerry and Joy—Thank you for your endless love and support, and for teaching us all about life, love, and justice. I am forever thankful for you and I'm beyond blessed to be your daughter.

To my sisters, Ashley and Danielle—You are my bestest friends in the universe. So thankful for a lifetime of fun memories and so many more to come.

# Contents

*Acknowledgements* . . . . . . . . . . . . . . . . . . . . . . . . . . . . . . . . . . viii
*List of Figures* . . . . . . . . . . . . . . . . . . . . . . . . . . . . . . . . . . . . . . . x
*List of Tables* . . . . . . . . . . . . . . . . . . . . . . . . . . . . . . . . . . . . . . . xi
*Meet the Author* . . . . . . . . . . . . . . . . . . . . . . . . . . . . . . . . . . . . xii

1. Introduction: Vision of Equity and Advocacy
   for Multilingual Learners . . . . . . . . . . . . . . . . . . . . . . . . . . . . . . 1

2. Cultivating Multilingual Mindsets Across
   a School Community . . . . . . . . . . . . . . . . . . . . . . . . . . . . . . . . 38

3. Affirming and Honoring the Linguistic Identities
   of Our Students . . . . . . . . . . . . . . . . . . . . . . . . . . . . . . . . . . . . 62

4. Ensuring Equity and Access for Multilingual
   Learners at Tier 1 . . . . . . . . . . . . . . . . . . . . . . . . . . . . . . . . . . . 93

5. Interrupting Inequitable MTSS Tiered
   Interventions and "Problem-Solving" Structures . . . . . . . 131

6. Dismantling Barriers for Advanced, Gifted,
   Enrichment Access . . . . . . . . . . . . . . . . . . . . . . . . . . . . . . . . 151

7. Dismantling Oppressive Family Engagement
   Practices and Designing Equitable Supports . . . . . . . . . . . 166

8. Upholding Our Commitments to Equity for
   Multilingual Learners and Families . . . . . . . . . . . . . . . . . . 188

   *References* . . . . . . . . . . . . . . . . . . . . . . . . . . . . . . . . . . . . . . . 196

# Acknowledgements

To my husband Eric—I cannot put into words how much I love you and how unbelievably thankful I am to be your wife. I hope our kids one day have partners who always lift them up, cheer them on, and help them cross the finish line. Thank you for letting me cry and for picking me back up and getting me back into the work. I love you.

To my kids TJ and Chloe—I love you beyond words! Thanks for being patient with me as I worked through this book.

Momma—this book simply would not exist without your heart, your voice, and your model of fighting for justice and serving others. I always want to make you proud, because I am so proud of you and who you are. You have the heart of a social justice warrior, and you invite others into the work along the way.

To "mine daddy"—you have always kept me going and knowing that you're in my corner cheering me on has meant the world to me. I always want to make you proud, because I am so proud of you and who you are. You have the biggest heart and your instinct to serve, support, and protect those around you is felt by everyone in our lives.

Ashley and Danielle—Thank you for never letting me cry alone. Thank you for celebrating all of life's moments and supporting me during my most difficult times. I am so thankful to have you as my best friends! So, Disney?

To my colleagues at the Illinois Resource Center—I'm so thankful to learn from each of you. I'm surrounded by brilliance and it keeps me growing and going! I cannot thank you enough for being such an incredible team, all eager to inspire, equip, and elevate our field. Thank you for your support, passion, and encouragement. Adelicia Brienzo—thank you for being my work bestie and for all of the donuts and coffee to help sustain me throughout this process! You always have just the right thing to say, and your kindness and support is deeply appreciated!

To my feedback crew and colleagues who've shared testimonials—I'm endlessly thankful! Dr. Denise Furlong and Dorina Sackman-Ebuwa—your friendship means the world to me! #WomenSupportingWomen! Alex Valencic and Tracy Fuentes, thanks for your friendship and support always! Jessica Reed and Bethany Cravin-Gale—thank you both so much! Valerie Peña Hernández—you are a true Advocate for Equity!

To all the teachers, assistants, leaders, coordinators, directors, and other school staff across the country who have contributed to this field in the name of equity and justice for multilingual learners and families—we are all in this together. I'm thankful for you and I'm so inspired by you. Let's keep going!

Special thank you to my friends and support system: Karina Paul (let's hit Kendra Scott soon!), Christina Cooper, Zully Zamora, Katya Nayman Chen, Taylor Ortiz, Amy Ziemann (we need to have a Lisa Frank Club meeting STAT), Dr. Denise Furlong, Dr. Dorina Sackman-Ebuwa, Jody Nolf, Dr. Carol Salva, and so many others. Thank you to all my Edu Heros in the field who have inspired me so deeply over the years. Please keep shining, as your light keeps us going!

To the students I've had the privilege of working with over the course of my career—I believe in you. You can do hard things. You can work really hard. You keep going when things are tough. You can get help when you need it. Your teachers believe in you. We love you and care about you. You are important. You are loved. You will do amazing things!

To the families I've had the privilege of partnering with over the course of my career—thank you for loving your babies. Thank you for all of the love you've poured into your families. Thank you for our laughs, our tears, our time, and our memories. I will always continue to cheer on your babies, and I will always cheer YOU on, too.

# Figures

1.1 Change agents don't tiptoe. They stomp. In stilettos. ...13
2.1 An example of two books that demonstrate linguistic oppression, and later linguistic empowerment. ...48
4.1 A sample of hold-up tools for a This or That structure. ...105
4.2 Sample listening guide that can accompany a This or That structure. This becomes a linguistic scaffold that carries into the next learning experience that can support multiple language domains. ...107
4.3 Spot It!. ...108
4.4 Sample co-constructed vocabulary tool bank. ...110
4.5 Sample content-specific Spot It game created from a generator. The generator can be found at https://macrusher.github.io/dobble-generator/. ...111
4.6 Sample of a Word Phrase Sentence Question (WPSQ) chart. ...114
7.1 Tweet from Kirsten Mulrooney that shows the power of social media for family engagement. ...177

# Tables

1.1 Refugees, Asylum Seekers, and Migrants . . . . . . . . . . . . . . . 26
1.2 Question, Equip, Act (Chapter 1) . . . . . . . . . . . . . . . . . . . . . . 36
2.1 Five Things to Say to Students to Invite
    Languages into the Classroom . . . . . . . . . . . . . . . . . . . . . . . . 58
2.2 Books that Highlight Multilingual Mindsets . . . . . . . . . . . . 59
2.3 Question, Equip, Act (Chapter 2) . . . . . . . . . . . . . . . . . . . . . . 60
3.1 Books that Highlight the Importance of
    Our Names. . . . . . . . . . . . . . . . . . . . . . . . . . . . . . . . . . . . . . . . . 69
3.2 Books That Feature Various Multilingual
    Identities and Experiences. . . . . . . . . . . . . . . . . . . . . . . . . . . . 91
3.3 Question, Equip, Act (Chapter 3) . . . . . . . . . . . . . . . . . . . . . . 92
4.1 Sample Translation Protocol for Instructional
    Purposes to Support Newcomer Students Using
    Three Prongs: Strategic, Translation, AND . . . . . . . . . . . . . 119
4.2 Question, Equip, Act (Chapter 4) . . . . . . . . . . . . . . . . . . . . . 130
5.1 Potential Questions for Multilingual Data Retreat. . . . . . . 140
5.2 Question, Equip, Act (Chapter 5) . . . . . . . . . . . . . . . . . . . . . 149
6.1 Question, Equip, Act (Chapter 6) . . . . . . . . . . . . . . . . . . . . . 165
7.1 Question, Equip, Act (Chapter 7) . . . . . . . . . . . . . . . . . . . . . 187

# Meet the Author

Carly Spina has almost two decades of experience in multilingual education, including her service as an EL (English language) teacher, a third-grade bilingual classroom teacher, and a district-wide multilingual instructional coach. Throughout her  work in education, she has supported students and families across over 70 languages. Spina has supported various program models including transitional programs of instruction, transitional bilingual programs, and dual language programs. She has implemented support for students through a variety of delivery models, including co-teaching, in-class support, and out-of-class support. She believes passionately that multilingual educators are partners with every role in the school ecosystem.

She is currently a multilingual education specialist at the Illinois Resource Center, providing professional learning opportunities and technical assistance support to educators and leaders across the state. Spina provides professional learning opportunities to schools and districts across the country, and is eager to support schools in Igniting Real Change for multilingual students and families. She enjoys networking and connecting with teachers and leaders. Her first book, *Moving Beyond for Multilingual Learners*, was a 2023 Equity in Excellence Award Winner.

Spina grew up in Chicago and now lives in the suburbs with her husband, two children, two dogs, and whatever foster puppies are currently receiving some love. She enjoys spending time with her family, reading, shopping, and wearing lots and lots of pink.

# 1

# Introduction
## Vision of Equity and Advocacy for Multilingual Learners

"I can't keep having this same conversation with the same people about this anymore. I'm done." I remember vividly saying this to my husband after an exceedingly difficult day at work. He watched as I collapsed in a heap on the couch, covering my face with my hands as if I could hold in all of the tears I had been suppressing all week. The tears fell anyway. My husband sat with me, and let me sob it all out. "I just can't. I don't think I have anything left to say or do to change anything. Nothing will ever change." I resigned myself to cry on the couch for the remainder of the evening while our two kids, our two dogs, and our two foster puppies bopped and hopped and danced and jumped all around us. Our townhouse was small and very, *very* full. That night, like many other similar nights, it felt extra full—like it couldn't possibly contain the entirety of all my huge emotions.

The next morning, I woke up early for work with very puffy eyes, and I helped my kids get ready for school and day care. After dropping them each off, I marched myself right back into the same place to have the same conversation with the same people.

Wash. Rinse. Repeat.
Fight. Cry. Collapse.
Wake up, get ready, do it again.

    During that particular night, the exhaustion was real. I had become frustrated earlier that day when an administrator that I mostly got along with had basically declared at a large staff meeting that "certain families we serve really don't care about these things, so it's on us." When I tried to interject to express my concern with his statement, he doubled down and dismissed me. I sat there, huffing and puffing and rolling my eyes. I vowed to follow up with this in writing so that this would be documented. I sat in my chair, blood boiling. Then I felt guilty for just sitting there rolling my eyes, because that's not going to do too much to change anything.

    At the end of that staff meeting, I was on my way back to my classroom when my cell phone rang. It was the mom of a student I served. She was telling me that the bus route still hadn't changed from a week ago, after she first told me about a problem where she felt uncomfortable having her student cross a busy street alone with no crossing guard on duty. Because this mom and I shared a language (Spanish) that our transportation department didn't share, I made sure the previous week that I sent an email and made a phone call to the central office so that I could share this mom's concerns. I was told by the person I spoke to that the problem was going to be resolved right away, and that the mom would be sent new bus route pickup information by the end of the following day. That obviously didn't happen. I felt guilty for not following up with this mom. I felt guilty for not checking in with the transportation director. I felt frustrated that no one in the district office spoke Spanish to be able to support this mom and help her with her very valid concern.

    Moments later (this is all still before any students came in for the day, mind you), a staff member from food services stopped by to deliver "low balance alert" letters for certain students in my class. I knew of two particular students in my class who were about to receive such notices whose families couldn't afford this right now, and even though I expressed this to the person, I was told that we don't make the rules, we just follow them. When she left, I pulled those letters off to the side, knowing that I was going to have to figure out how to pay those balances without this woman knowing. This wasn't the first time we'd had this discussion, and I knew it wouldn't be the last. The year prior, I had just thrown my hands up and decided I'd figure out how to pay those balances myself because the arguments that we'd get into just didn't feel worth the energy (even though, years later, it still brings me immense shame that I didn't do more, say more, or take more action).

Later that day, I sat at a data meeting over lunch, where my colleagues and I shared spreadsheets across all of our third grade students. At the time, I was the third grade classroom teacher in our bilingual program. I was teaching math in Spanish that year, with bridging lessons into English at the end of each unit. Even though instruction was in Spanish, my students were being assessed in math in English, just like all the monolingual students in third grade. The folks who were facilitating the meeting had pulled all the third grade math data and highlighted certain students in different colors to indicate their need for extra support. When we got to my class's data review at the meeting, almost every row on the spreadsheet had my students highlighted in a different color. My colleagues looked at me, some looking horrified, and others looking empathetic. Some said things like, "Well, there's only going up from here, right! They're going to grow so much!" I reminded the folks around the table that our current district language allocation plan meant that students studied math in Spanish almost exclusively over their earlier elementary years, so an English math assessment doesn't quite capture their true story. I shared that during our last unit test, most of my students showed mastery of the standards. Glances were exchanged, and there were murmurings of "oh, yes, *of course*." Yet the rows and rows of my students remained highlighted on the spreadsheet to suggest that they weren't "on track." I left the meeting feeling frustrated, unheard, and defeated. After I walked back to my classroom to put down my laptop and turned to walk out to pick up my students from recess, one of my colleagues stopped by my room and said that they'd be happy to work with any of my students who needed extra help.

Have you had those moments, too? Those days, weeks, months... years? As I talk with educators and leaders, these and others are moments that keep occurring and recurring. Years later, I reflect on these seasons of defeat and overwhelm when facing systems that treated my students and families unfairly. I reflect on those moments of being told that all I did was complain, and how several folks would tell me throughout the years that I needed to be more positive, or be more of a team player since we're all just trying our best. I also reflect on all the ways I didn't advocate like maybe I should have—and that brings me the biggest shame of all. Why didn't I do more? Why didn't I take more action? Then I grapple with more frustration about how I felt like it had to be just up to me to advocate—why did fighting for equity have to be the job of just one person?

There are still days when I doubt if any words or actions or decisions or conversations will make a difference. Then there are days when I see how words, actions, decisions, and conversations DO make a difference. That keeps me going.

My hope in writing this book is that we can dive deeper into actionable equity for multilingual learners and families. I hope that this can serve as an opportunity for honest moments of reflection for ourselves and each other. I'm hopeful that we can unpack all of the work that goes into advocacy for those we serve. Ultimately, I hope this can equip you with tools as you fight for equity for our students.

Before we get started, let's unpack two terms that will be used throughout this work: *equity* and *advocacy*. Let's first begin with equity.

To get real about equity, we have to acknowledge the inequities that already exist. In the examples I shared earlier, there were several inequities that directly impacted the students and families that I served. For example, deficit-laden beliefs of leaders that positioned certain families as somehow "less informed," "less involved," or "less-educated" were shared with staff regularly. This inequity reinforced to all staff negative mindsets, beliefs, and stereotypes of the families we served. The language access of families to be able to share transportation concerns was quite limited due to our lack of multilingual staff and a lack of a clear pathway for both families and staff in gaining language access to and for all. This inequity provides more access to information to English language users and less access to users of other languages. The "low balance" alerts that were often sent in English to families routinely on certain days of the week didn't take into account that certain families struggled with paying.

> Yes, even though there were free/reduced breakfast and lunch forms that families might be able to fill out (if families have the time, the language, the literacy, the confidence, and the trust of the school and state to fill out those forms)—even so, some families do not qualify for free/reduced meals and still struggle to pay the low-balance alerts on breakfast/lunch accounts. And, as a side note, as a mom who had a degree and multiple jobs, I ALSO struggled with paying bills and feeding my kids sometimes, and the lengths I took to hide that from the world eventually caught up with me. The shame is still there.

The inequities here prioritize students and families who have socioeconomic privilege and food security. When I had to attend data meeting after data meeting that suggested that my multilingual students were behind while monolingual students were ahead of them, even though our bilingual program was structured differently but was still being assessed through an English monolingual lens, it fueled conversations about how "low-achieving" my students were.

These were all examples of inequities that existed within the system at that time. I know there are many, many more that aren't mentioned in these scenarios. These were just some of the more obvious ones that popped up a little louder on that specific day.

I also want to acknowledge the inequities that existed in these scenarios *as the teacher* serving multilingual students and families—this is important to acknowledge, because ultimately it impacts multilingual students and families.

As a teacher, the data meetings made me feel like my instruction wasn't up to par with that of my colleagues across the school building, even though I was attending more professional learning than they were, as I had all of their mandated professional learning plus the additional layers of multilingual curriculum, instruction, and assessment. This meant more time out of the classroom, and more time devoted to writing subplans. This was inequitable to me as a teacher, and also inequitable to my students.

As a teacher, the number of times that I had been pulled to either interpret or translate for the families I served far exceeded the "typical" expectations of communication home. For example, monolingual teachers serving monolingual students never had to serve as a go-between or language broker between families and folks at the transportation department. It was expected that I would do this because I was the bilingual classroom teacher. This extra layer of work wasn't compensated. The additional workload of communication back and forth multiple ways, plus all of the follow-ups, was inequitable to me as a teacher, and also inequitable to my families. Monolingual families could simply call the transportation office because they had language access.

Additionally, the shame I experienced about not being a strong enough or good enough advocate still haunts me to this day—and I know I mentioned that specific word a few times already. The guilt and shame were always there, in each of the scenarios. The guilt and shame that I carried around felt like an unspoken and invisible weight, but I know personally how it impacted my mental, physical, spiritual, and financial health. I believe that this guilt and shame contributed to a faster burnout rate than my colleagues. I often felt powerless, unheard, defeated, scared, anxious, and hopeless. Please note that this is not to suggest this is how I always felt every single day—because a lot of good things happened, too—which I will also share throughout this book.

If we have folks in school systems that are trying to push their systems to be more equitable for students and families, how do we care for them? How do we ensure that they're feeling supported in their work, and that they're not burning out? Care and sustainability of our people are two critical pieces of equity.

We've seen the graphics that have been shared on the internet with variations of young folks viewing a baseball game over a fence. Some of us have also gone on to explore how trying to simplify such a complex issue in one graphic representation can also be harmful to marginalized groups based on how privileged groups view and interpret the image.

What might be a privileged point of view? First, I want to acknowledge that the term "privilege" can make some folks feel itchy, especially if they themselves have benefited from some type of privilege. In our earlier examples, language privilege is a big one. Language privilege, here specifically, English language privilege, is one that many of us (especially if we are monolingual English users in the US) often don't acknowledge or recognize because we don't regularly experience or haven't ever experienced what it's like to not have shared language access. Please note that this is different from having empathy after traveling abroad (which is another privilege) and experiencing a week of difficulty communicating with the community around you, like a visit to a restaurant. One's travel abroad experiences may have brought an opportunity for developing empathy for others, specifically for the language needs of multilingual students and families, but one still might not fully understand the entirety of English language privilege in the US for students and families, especially in schools.

If we were to take the graphic of the folks viewing the baseball game through the fence, we might simply suggest having interpreters or translations available as "the solution" to the scenario about the mom sharing her concerns about the bus. However, there is a larger nuance to that (we'll get to this in Chapter 7).

Can equity for multilingual learners be treated as an initiative? In schools and districts across the country, we begin tons and tons (and umm, TONS) of rollouts for new initiatives. We pour countless resources into new initiatives via time, energy, funding, and materials. Similarly, we also drop initiatives as soon as something "bigger" or "more pressing" comes along, such as new curricular resources, new state- or district-level policies, new standards, or a new leader with a new vision enters the system. Have you seen this, too? I remember laughing with a fellow veteran colleague once when our system adopted a new English Language Arts resource. She said something to the tune of, "We have to listen to this company's rep read us this slide deck about how to redesign our entire instructional framework. The district spent tens of thousands of dollars on this, and I know it'll be gone in five years."

Dang.

Have you been there, too? Initiatives are everywhere. If you were to list out your system's current initiatives, how many might there be right now for you? How many of the ones you've listed have been the same for the last few years? How many are brand new? How many do you foresee will remain in five years' time?

Even while most of us can acknowledge the sometimes-fleeting presence of initiatives, equity for our students is often treated as something that "comes and goes" depending on who's in charge, or who from the school community is outraged enough to douse any efforts in this area.

I used to feel so excited when a new equity team or committee would be formed in my community because I felt like we would finally have some momentum, energy, and dedication to this work. As the months would go by, there would be a tool, a product, or a resource shared out with various stakeholders. I would again get very excited and optimistic that change would occur! Then, inevitably, the efforts would fizzle out. Someone might leave the team. The grant runs out of funds. People get burned out. The team faces opposition from a board member or community member. And it would eventually disappear.

Perhaps the term "initiative" is where my word association bias comes into play. We all associate words with different meanings based on our own experiences and understandings. As a longtime educator myself, I know that I associate different words with different experiences. For example, when "collaboration time" became an initiative in my local school district, that eventually meant "unpaid two-hour meetings after school every two weeks." Ugh. Maybe you've had this misfortune, too? This ended up costing me more money in childcare and less take-home pay. For that reason, the experience behind that word negatively influenced my association with it. Perhaps that is what's happening here as well. Do you have another example of a word-association bias in education?

When I hear and see "initiative," my own brain interprets it as a "current fad that will drive a lot of initial resources and energy that will eventually disappear." While I want to recognize that a starting point or an initial launch/plan/study is necessary, I struggle with the word "initiative."

The problem with treating equity as an initiative is that eventually it becomes less of a priority for someone in the district or system. Initiatives are dependent on leadership support, community support, funding, and implementation. How many of our school- or district-based initiatives result in lasting change? We must address the false comfort in finding "an equity solution" in the form of creating a committee, a tool like a flowchart, or even naming one difficult conversation "our equity plan." While these all sound like they may lead to a few positive outcomes for a few folks, we aren't getting to the heart of the work if we are just focused on the formation of a team or the creation of a product.

Equity for multilingual learners is not an initiative. It's not a theme for a school year. It's not a committee. It's not a one-day workshop. True equity for multilingual learners is interwoven into the fabric of everything we do. It has a dedicated time, space, and presence in each facet of our work with students, families, and each other. It is evident in our unit design. It is present in our instruction and assessment practices. It is alive in our decision making.

If your school leadership is too scared to even utter the word "equity," we have a larger problem.

Some districts today are fearful to even begin this work because equity has become a bad word. School boards have threatened teachers, principals, and other school staff members from engaging in conversations. All DEI (diversity-equity-inclusion) work in schools is actually banned in some states. People have been fired from their positions because they've pointed out systems that privilege some over others. Teachers have been fired for teaching accurate history. Librarians have been fired for the books they keep in the library. There are some states where teachers had to pack up all of their classroom books so that someone "with authority" can "approve" them before any students were allowed to even have access to them.

If you are currently serving in those places and spaces, our hearts break for you. I cannot imagine. If you're still picking up this book and continuing to pursue your professional and personal growth in this area, we are all cheering you on. If this isn't representative of your state or your district, and you are eager to dig into this work, we are all also cheering you on. However, let's remember that treating equity as a checklist or an initiative isn't going to lead to any transformational change in your system.

Another challenge in this arena is that many communities pose equity work as something that interested stakeholders can choose to support. As in, it's optional. As in, those who are "ready" to engage in conversations have a space to do so, and those who "aren't ready" or uninterested don't have to engage with the work. This is incredibly problematic. While I can recognize that each human being has different levels of prior learning, exposures, lived experiences, and different interests or passions, we cannot (CANNOT) continue to allow folks who work with our children to opt out. Equity for our students cannot be optional. The students in our schools and districts cannot afford for you to wait until your staff or community is "ready" to have conversations about equity.

Additionally, for each of us as individuals, regardless of where our school or district is within this work, we must consider our own levels of commitment. We have to be honest and recognize our own moments of weakness. We have to be able to lean fully into uncomfortable moments where we either consciously or unconsciously opted out. Or perhaps, based on our own identity, positionality, or proximity to a situation/conversation/event/moment, we turned our attention away. For example, if I'm a believer in equity for all students, but my heart and mind is very aware of how I advocate for equity for multilingual students, do I still bring that same energy if a colleague shares a consideration about equity for transgender students? My passion for equity shouldn't be situational, and sometimes, our individual realities (again, perhaps due to our own identity, positionality, or proximity to a situation) might reveal that *my passion for equity is situational*. Uh oh!

Furthermore, what is my level of commitment when someone pushes back? Maybe I'll continue to feel driven by my vision for equity when I'm disagreeing with a teammate down the hall, but what happens when it's my boss or evaluator who disagrees with me? What happens if I'm brought up by our local board of education—will my commitment waiver? *Carly, I can't lose my job! I have bills to pay!*

Equity for multilingual learners cannot be championed by one individual, one team, or one department. We cannot expect one human being or one small group of human beings to be the only ones committed to this work. This is not sustainable. This is not fair to the adults who are engaging in this work. Most importantly, this is not fair to the students and families we serve. Imagine being the multilingual students who are in the second grade teacher's class—the teacher who has largely been uninterested in equity for her multilingual students, and has been allowed by the school building or district to abdicate responsibility or opt out. What of that teacher? *What about those students?!*

This takes hard and fast dedication and commitment from the decision-makers. Equity requires advocacy.

## Advocacy

Advocacy calls each of us to examine our own personal and social identities and positionalities and leverage our positions, knowledge, expertise, and voice. To be an advocate we have to consider our places and spaces that we serve within, and how we can use those places and spaces to either step in, speak up, or act out when needed. For some of us, this means exploring how we can leverage our various privileges, if we have certain privileges. Some of us might need to step up in bigger ways.

Advocates have to reckon with the fact that equity work requires discomfort. Too often we prioritize the feelings and "sensitivities" of those with privilege. For example, in a neighboring school district near my home, there was a small group of educators who came together to do a book study on the book titled *This Book Is Anti-Racist* by Tiffany Jewell. They were really feeling energized at the conclusion of their book study. They wanted to do a presentation to their local board of education to share their personal reflections, connections, and opportunities for staff to engage in anti-racism work. They reached out to the board without letting their principal know first. Before they knew it, they were (literally) called into the principal's office and were basically told that because all of the board members were white, they felt like this book study idea was an attack on their individual and collective character. They were absolutely offended at the invitation to participate in this book study. The principal shared that any future efforts to engage in anti-racist work should be cleared through him first, "because there's a process we must follow." The team felt frustrated and pointed out the "commitment to equity" statement within the district's strategic plan. The principal doubled down and said that this work is probably going to have to happen several years down the road: "The board already feels overwhelmed with this referendum passing. They just want to focus on that right now. I don't think that adding this to their plate will feel very good. They do a lot of good and we don't want them to feel uncomfortable."

Sheesh.

We can't ask the folks who are ready to champion this work in their schools to "be soft" or "be gentle" with their expectations for the system. Equity work cannot rely on "nice folks" tiptoeing around stubborn privileged folks. *Walk on eggshells! Tiptoe! Don't cause trouble!* In the above example, we were prioritizing the feelings of the white board members instead of the impact on students and families.

Change agents don't tiptoe. They stomp. In stilettos. In sneakers. In their favorite boots. I happen to stomp in my stilettos that are pink and sparkly. In fact, I keep my pink and sparkly stilettos in my office every day on a shelf where I can see them. Whenever I do a livestream or record a virtual session from my office, you'll likely see them sitting there, on the top shelf. I keep them visible, because some days I need that reminder that I should not tiptoe. I've done plenty of that in the past. Yes—actual tiptoeing.

**FIGURE 1.1** Change agents don't tiptoe. They stomp. In stilettos. Photograph by the author.

Let's go ahead and address this real-life TipToe.

As a first year teacher, I was so excited to meet my students. My official title was "English Learner Teacher," or EL Teacher, which meant that I would be serving and supporting students across three grade levels who were learning English as an additional language (sometimes it was their second or third language, and sometimes English was a language they were learning at the same time as their heritage language of their families). Most of my students spoke languages like Spanish, Korean, Mongolian, Polish, and Russian, but there were over 60 languages in the community at that time. Sometimes my students were born in the community, and had been speaking English and their other language for their whole lives. Other students I served were brand new to the country, community, and to the English language.

My job was to support their language growth and development in English across all different content areas, like English language arts (reading/writing), math, science, and social studies. I was told to modify work, lessons, quizzes, and assessments to make it "simpler and easier for my students to understand." Because I had just finished student teaching, and I had just learned about all the different models of supporting multilingual students, I wondered if I'd be co-teaching with classroom teachers, or if I'd be pulling students out of class for a "resource" block so that I could help them individually or in smaller groups, or if I'd be pushing into various classrooms and supporting students. When I asked this question, the answer was actually surprising.

The TipToe has entered the chat.

When I was first hired as an EL teacher, I was expected to literally tiptoe into classrooms and support students in secret. No, seriously: "Just try to sneak in and quietly help the students who need it!" I felt like a cartoon character. I was expected to literally whisper support to students so that other students wouldn't get distracted. I was expected to pull "my kids" to the BACK TABLE to "help" them. Can we unpack this for just a second? Take a deep breath, friends, because this one always gets me really riled up.

The "my kids" vs. "our kids" conversation continues to pop up in schools across the country. I appreciate reflective language practices that help us to call attention to the way we use our language and how what we say often is a representation of what we believe. If any one of us teaches in a school, we must operate under the belief that every student is our student—yes, even students who aren't in my classroom or on my roster this year. Phrases we should consider retiring include "your kids" or "my kids"—because *each student* of the school deserves *each teachers'* commitment, attention, effort, and energy.

The expectation or assumption that I must pull "my kids" to the back of the classroom is also grossly troubling. Where I support students (physically in any space) actually does matter, but there's a lot to unpack here. If we teach students at a small group table, that doesn't necessarily mean it's a bad thing. Perhaps that's where we keep supplies and materials. Perhaps that table offers better proximity and more optimal space for peer-to-peer conversations. Again—a small group table isn't automatically bad. The issue comes when one adult says or implies that the other adult (and "their" students) should be removed in order to not distract other students (and perhaps the other students we are fearful of distracting are students who have English language privilege). If the back of the classroom is the best place to learn for specific reasons, fine—but if the back of the classroom is a way to "remove" students to prioritize the needs of other students, that's worrisome. We might also consider if what we're doing with students would also benefit other students (hint: it would, but more on that later). When one group of students always sees the same students moving to the back of the room to receive support, what does that do to their understanding of the world? How does that impact how they see themselves or their peers as learners?

Let's also examine the whispering expectation in this scenario. If, as the teacher, I'm expected to not be seen or heard by anyone else in class, why am I there in the first place? My work is quite literally silenced—which means my efforts to serve students is also silenced. For a student group that has been historically silenced and marginalized in schools (down to the right to even be in the same school as their peers due to their descent, their immigration status, and their language—we'll talk about specific court cases about each of these in our next chapter), this is unacceptable. Later in this book, we'll explore other ways that this silencing has occurred when we discuss linguistic oppression. Get ready!

Let me also acknowledge that this wasn't the expectation or even the "vibe" in all classrooms. I had many colleagues who were absolutely eager to collaborate to best support our students—and I'm thankful for them and for folks like them every single day.

As the certified educator with the teaching license and coinciding endorsement, my expertise should've mattered in that above TipToe situation. However, I was also up against the attitudes, beliefs, and practices of colleagues who were *not* interested or willing to collaborate or offer shared time and space—and this made me feel inferior. The not-yet-unpacked layer of imposter syndrome weighed too heavily on me at the time to fully embody my skills and knowledge. *I'm still so new to this profession. They've been doing this forever. Who am I to offer any insights here?* Instead of utilizing my skills (even though they were still very much developing!), I allowed several classrooms to impose that demand on me to tiptoe and whisper.

Have you had that moment where you've doubted your own expertise? Perhaps you've had doubts about your level of knowledge or your skillset. I know I still struggle with this, all these years later. Were you ever made to feel like you were "too new" to a school or classroom or content area to contribute? It's not a fun experience.

Does this mean that my colleagues are bad people? No, not necessarily. All of us in education (myself included here, folks) often engage in practices that we've inherited over the years without anyone questioning it or offering an alternative. Remember, *I went along with this*. Not acknowledging my own skills, not growing my own professional skillset, not equipping myself with tools to combat change, not offering an alternative, not asking a simple question, not standing up for students or myself—all of my non-actions here show that I am guilty as well. I allowed this to happen—and for longer than I'd like to admit.

Have you had those moments, too? Has there been a moment where you've gone along with something that you knew was harmful to students, either due to lack of confidence to speak out, or out of fear of offending a colleague? What might be something that you witnessed that you didn't call out? Was there something that a colleague said or shared with you that you knew was harmful to the social-emotional well-being of a student?

Friend, I'm here still owning up to stuff. I'm not here to judge anyone. I'm on this journey, too. I want us to take this journey together. I can't preach about this without being honest with myself, with you, or others around me.

Let's go back to my first year as the English Learner Teacher—I was not equipped. I didn't question anything. I didn't move the needle.

Now that I engage often in reflection, I wish I could have a conversation with my younger teacher-self. I would want her to look at this through a more reflective lens with deeper layers of context. I would equip her with some history, and remind her of how multilingual learners have been historically marginalized and silenced. I would encourage her to ask questions about why this might be the expectation about how so many classrooms seemed to run in that system. I would challenge her to identify how to change this situation. I would ask her to watch her students' faces as they watched the adult who was supposed to advocate for them, teach them, and care for them . . . *whisper*. The silencing and the whispering—they both scream at me today. Loudly. It makes me feel ashamed.

If you were to write a letter to your teacher self from a few years ago, what might you say? What advice would you gently pass to younger you? What might be some words of wisdom that younger you could hold onto about the importance of advocacy and equity for the students in our care? Hey reader, take a moment and write that letter. Seriously.

Shame and guilt are hard. These feelings are enough for many of us to turn away. It feels like wading knee-deep in mud or quicksand. We want to move and take steps forward but the negative feelings seem to hold us in place, slowing us down or stopping us completely.

For me, I can acknowledge the saying "when you know better, you do better." As I was new to the profession, I wasn't yet equipped with the tools, the language, the self-advocacy skills, or the confidence to speak up and speak out. How could I have possibly had all of that right out of college and student teaching? I never entered this profession to cause harm—I wanted to put good into the world! I love kids! I spent a lot of time reflecting on my own beliefs about education and making a positive impact. I was a nice young woman with good intentions! Yes, this is leading right to a conversation about intent and impact.

No, I never wanted to cause harm. AND. . . it is also possible that *my colleagues also never wanted to cause harm.* While my privileged mindset might want me to believe that there are NO educators or leaders who hate kids and want them to suffer, I also need to listen to and respect the lived experiences of students, colleagues, families, and others around me. So, of course, I've worked with a lot of burnt out, grumpy, degraded, stubborn folks. I've also been a burnt out, grumpy, degraded, and stubborn educator myself! Even so, someone I serve alongside might share that their experiences in different classrooms and/or work environments felt particularly harmful or unsafe for them. This is a harsh reality for my privilege to recognize, especially when I want things to "feel good" or I just really, really want to believe that "we're all here for the kids!" I have to be a little more real here. While I want to give my colleagues (and myself!) the benefit of the doubt, harm is harm. Period. Even if the harm wasn't intended—it's still harm. It is possible to have good intentions but also have a negative impact. It is also entirely possible that an educator treats certain students (and/or colleagues) differently because of blatant racism, or implicit bias. This is why it's so important to have a framework in which to do this work—I will be introducing my framework later in this chapter!

Remember that TipToe? Well, the TipToe also happens at decision-making tables. While it is important to honor each person's individual journey, we can't settle for "good enough" or "close enough" equity. What does this mean? This happens when folks "compromise" on actions to ease the tension or placate a person with privilege and power.

## Voices from the Field

### Dr. Denise Furlong, Author of Voices of Newcomers

As educators we must be sure to not to consider our own perspectives over those of the learners and families we serve. We don't want our voices to overcome those of the community. I've met many well-meaning educators who fought for services or

> benefits on behalf of learners' families—but never asked the families if they wanted those things. Even though we may feel strongly about things for the learners and families we serve, true advocates amplify voices rather than make decisions for others. To do so would suggest that our judgment is more sound than that of others. We work alongside all stakeholders and truly listen to their voices; our voices should never drown out the voices of the community.

## False Advocates

We also have to be weary of folks who call themselves advocates but are actually conducting disguised white saviorism. It might look and sound like advocacy at surface level, but sometimes we have to look deeper.

For example, I know a teacher who often refers to their students' immigration stories, or their students' personal hardship stories, as "our story." It rubs me the wrong way, because it's not this teacher's story! It's theirs. Exploiting the stories of our students and families is not advocacy.

This teacher may have had some elements of "positive intent" here. This teacher may be trying to elevate and amplify students' lived experiences in an effort to build a general sense of awareness or build empathy amongst educators. However, the impact is that this teacher is claiming a narrative that is not theirs to claim.

Another teacher I know often shares one specific story about how they helped their students navigate a very complex traumatic situation. Perhaps they share this story in an effort to show other educators ways to be supportive of students and families they serve. However, the impact is that this teacher (who is white) positions themselves as the hero in this family's trauma because of all the things they did to support them during that difficult time.

Positioning oneself (while white) as the hero of a minoritized student or family is saviorism. White saviorism is not advocacy.

## Throwing the Flag

Advocates speak up and speak out. We praise the good work and we denounce the work that poses obstacles for some while privileging others. Advocacy can mean, sometimes, waving a red flag.

Growing up in Chicago as a kid, I'd watch many Chicago Bears football games with my dad. He'd spend Sunday mornings down the block at our local park in Lincoln Square with other guys from the neighborhood. They'd play flag football in the park for around two hours. Sometimes I'd run down the block to meet them on the days we skipped church and I'd bring a handful of Pepsi cans (no one cared about hydration back then, I'm serious) and we'd all walk back together. The guys would all part ways, my dad would shower and change into his clean Bears jersey, and he'd set up his jar of peanuts or cheese popcorn or pork rinds (and yet another Pepsi) to watch the Bears game. I'd sometimes sit on the floor and pretend to watch while playing Barbies, solitaire, or doing homework. Every now and then my sisters and I would join in "doing dad's hair" so pretty with our colorful barrettes and clips while he'd watch the game.

My dad has always been a devoted Bears fan. He was passionate about his Bears and he'd often yell lots of fun, colorful phrases at the TV each game, including "GO BABY, GO!" during an offensive run, and "THAT'S WHAT I'M TALKING ABOUT!" during other exciting moments. He'd have the players' backs every single play, and he was ready to throw down with the refs when he thought they had missed a foul against the Bears. He'd angrily yell, "COME ON! THROW THE FLAG!" along with some other choice words I won't mention here.

Now that we're all adults, we still watch lots of Bears games together on Sundays. My sister Ashley and I will still lock eyes and laugh when Dad yells out, "THROW THE FLAG!"

During my years in education, I have been an active observer of processes that serve students and families well. For example, when I see a content teacher sitting side-by-side planning for instruction with the multilingual teacher, I excitedly cheer on those moments with my own internal "GO BABY, GO!" When I hear a teacher say, "No, we don't have to simplify the language everywhere, we can enhance the current text with some additional entry points like synonyms and visuals," you may see me jumping up and down and shouting, "THAT'S WHAT I'M TALKING ABOUT!"

And so, as you might expect, I've also seen some moments where I witness foul play: educational malpractice, illegal practices, problematic mindsets that impact decision making, and much more. When I see the TipToe as the sole methodology of offering in-class "support" to multilingual students. When I hear the district office say they don't have the time or budget to translate an important piece of communication to the community. When a teacher calls their multilingual student "low." That's where my mom's social justice warrior spirit and my dad's fierce protective skills spiral me into a loud, booming, "THROW THE FLAG!"

I've seen a lot of funny Instagram and TikTok accounts that have folks running across my screen with either green flags or red flags, based on what stories are being shared by folks. For example, if someone shares a story of something kind that their significant other did for them, he'd stitch that video, so it cuts to him running in a field with a large, green flag. Check out creators like Dustin Poynter, @dustinpoynter on TikTok. These videos always make me laugh (or they really anger me, depending on the topic!). I think a lot of us in education have seen moments when we'd either individually or collectively wave a gigantic green flag to cheer on the great work happening—and we've also seen moments when we wish we could wave a gigantic red flag in someone's face.

Throughout this book, I'm going to share those red flag moments with a nod to my father's "THROW THE FLAG!" So when you see it, imagine me running in front of you, waving my gigantic red flag. Those red flags are practices that must be stopped immediately in order to promote more equitable outcomes for multilingual students and families.

Advocacy also recognizes those green flags as well. The green flags are waved just as enthusiastically for when things are going well. Someone is pushing back on a colleague who says that multilingual learners have no background knowledge. Someone is calling out bias by asking at a meeting whose experience is being centered in a specific text that the committee chose as their primary resource. Someone is calling out that the cost for the extracurricular activity is not affordable to every student and family in the system. A leader is willing to listen to a staff member sharing how the comment they made about families in our community was harmful, and thanked the staff member for sharing their concern, and assured a commitment to further growth. GREEN. FLAGS. BABY.

As advocates, we must pause and recognize the green flags just as much as the red flags, because the green flags fuel us. The green flags help us to identify other change makers, and sometimes these may come from the people or places we might least expect!

The hardest part about green flags is that sometimes we don't immediately see a giant, transformational change for the entire system as soon as that green flag is waved. For example, there may be a moment where a curriculum committee or team builds in linguistic scaffolds at the forefront of unit design before sending it out to the whole district. This feels amazing, because they're showing a commitment to honoring the linguistic needs of our multilingual students! We start to feel hopeful! However, when implementation rolls around, you find out that many classroom and content teachers are intentionally "skipping" those pieces of their instruction because they were overheard saying, "Well, I only have one multilingual student in my class, so I just taught it the way I've always taught it and didn't change anything."

That can absolutely feel frustrating. That can make the advocates feel a sense of defeat—but every green flag helps to drive the system forward, closer to what it needs to be. In the above example, let's celebrate that the curriculum committee came together and prioritized our students' needs at the initial level of work! In the past, perhaps the team would first share units with no linguistic support identified with the district staff and say, "Now you can tweak it for YOUR students!" So this moment can be a "both/and" situation. We can cheer on this team and thank them for their commitment, *and* we also can remain unwavering for our expectation of equity. Celebrate the good and continue driving forward.

In the above example, what might be one next step? Perhaps we can identify an implementation rollout that prioritizes the needs of every learner. Perhaps we come together during our weekly team meetings during that unit and discuss how we've utilized the scaffolds or the impact of the scaffolds. We must continue to identify our potential next steps forward. We cannot settle for scraps when it comes to equity. Our students deserve better. Our families deserve better.

> **Voices from the Field**
>
> ***Valerie Peña Hernández, Strategic Advisor for K-12 Curriculum and Instruction (Multilingual and Special Education Specialization)***
>
> The truth is, until we view ALL students as part of general education first, while embracing everything they bring to the table, nothing will truly change. Our current school systems are structured to see students primarily through the lens of interventions and disability labels, often defining them by their challenges instead of recognizing their wholeness.

## Students We Serve

Who do we serve? Let's talk about the term *multilingual learner*. As mentioned earlier, people often make associations to different words based on our experiences and exposures. If I say "multilingual learner," what images come to mind for you? Which students do you think of right away? It is important for folks in education to understand how diverse this group is. One thing I like to do when I work in schools and districts is that I ask everyone to draw a large beach umbrella and write inside of it MULTILINGUAL LEARNERS. Then, underneath, we break down specific student groups that are representative of the diversity of this very large group. This helps folks understand that this group is anything but homogenous.

> **Special Note**
>
> **Languaging** refers to how we each utilize our language skills through a combination of speaking, listening, reading, writing, and viewing. This also includes non-linguistic communication.
> **Languagers** refer to those who language across each domain. This also includes non-linguistic communication.

### Newcomers

Newcomer students are defined by the US Department of Education as students in K-12 who are within their first three years of education in the US. Even within this specific group of multilingual learners, there is a ton of diversity. Their proficiencies of their heritage language are quite varied. Some have heritage language oracy skills (speaking/listening), some have heritage literacy skills (reading/writing), some have both—and some have neither. Within their English languaging skills, it's the same (varied levels of oracy and literacy). Some newcomers arrive in our communities with multiple adult family members, and some arrive as unaccompanied minors. Some newcomers arrive with lots of familial connections within the community that can support them in finding housing, jobs, registering kids for school, filing paperwork, getting a cellular phone, and also connecting with any necessary social service agencies that can support their transition. Some arrive not knowing anyone, navigating a new community and a new language alone, and not having any connections to needed community resources.

Each newcomer student has their own journey of what brought them to the US. Some are very exciting stories, and some are incredibly tragic and heartbreaking. We cannot assume that all newcomers and families are arriving with trauma, although this is a very common assumption in schools.

Have you seen any horror movie where there's a killer on the loose who calls the victim to let them know that trouble is near? And in that movie, there's some voice somewhere that says, "The call is coming from inside the house!" Sometimes, as I often say in newcomer workshops that I lead, "the trauma is coming from inside the schoolhouse."

While we may never fully know or understand the lived experiences of our newcomer students before they arrive, we do have a certain amount of control over their lived experiences while at school. Newcomer students might experience direct racism from a classmate on the bus who tells them to "go back to where they came from." Newcomer students might experience exclusion from their math teacher who is unsure of how to scaffold their lesson and so they just say, "Here. You can just color this page while the rest of us do this math lesson," without any extra effort or care. Newcomer students might experience fear when trying to navigate an active shooter drill for the first time in a US school, because their home country never had anything like this and no teacher has sat down to explain to them what this is or why we must practice it, like we do for fire drills or tornado drills (sometimes as teachers, we assume that someone else either has or will explain some of these things, and it ends up being that no one does!). Sometimes, we are the ones causing the trauma. And that sucks. But let's own up to it.

Trauma is very dependent on a child's perception of a situation *and also* the amount of access to resources that can support them. How trauma presents itself is also very different from child to child.

Some of our newcomer students are refugees, asylum seekers, or migrants. Sometimes we use these terms interchangeably but they're actually different. See Table 1.1.

**TABLE 1.1** Refugees, Asylum Seekers, and Migrants

| | |
|---|---|
| Refugee | People who have been forced to leave their homes due to war, poverty, or violence. Refugees are protected by law. |
| Asylum Seeker | People who have left their homes to escape persecution, but are not (yet) legally recognized as a refugee. Seeking asylum is legal. |
| Migrant | People who have moved from one place to another for a variety of reasons, including economic reasons (like finding work) or to be with family. They may also have left due to war, poverty, or violence. |

Not all multilingual learners are newcomers. Many of the multilingual learners in the US were born in the United States. They also have unique language journeys. This group also has large variances of languaging skills in English and an additional language. Did you know that English might even be their "first" language? Yep! Let's explore other groups of multilingual learners under this large umbrella.

### "Long-Term English Learners"

Another group of multilingual learners is referred to in many states as *long-term English learners*, or LTELs. "Long-term" is used to represent the years of being in a multilingual learner program. Most states agree that after five years of formal instruction in US school within a multilingual learner program, the student is now identified as a "long-term English learner." For me, this term feels a little itchy, for a few reasons. The first reason is that deep levels of language take closer to 7–10 years of high-quality language instruction to develop. Second, it seems to be a term that criticizes the learner rather than address the system's accountability. This is one of the most misunderstood groups in schools, especially in middle schools and high schools. Teachers and leaders often erroneously assume that "something must be wrong" if a student doesn't receive a magical state-created score on an annual language assessment by year 6. Rather than investigating whether or not the student has been given high-quality linguistically appropriate support and instruction, they supply an additional label to the student. This student group varies in proficiency levels in English and their additional language(s).

### Dually Identified Learners
Dually Identified Learners refers to multilingual students with various learning abilities, disabilities, and learning needs, usually under an IEP (an Individualized Education Program). Districts are often disproportionate in how many IEPs in their system belong to multilingual learners—there is often either an overrepresentation or an underrepresentation. Schools need to shore up this process in order to ensure that all students' needs are being met through a linguistically and culturally appropriate lens.

### Gifted Multilingual Learners
Still another group is gifted multilinguals. Many teachers and leaders struggle with identifying gifted monolingual students, so adding the complexity of language learning sometimes makes folks in schools take a few additional stumbles in their understanding. Chapter 7 will go a little deeper into how we can identify and provide access to gifted programming for multilinguals.

### Students with Limited or Interrupted Formal Education
Students with limited or interrupted formal education, or SLIFE, is yet another group of multilingual learners. These are often newcomer students who have had interruptions of either several weeks, months, or years. These interruptions can be due to many reasons including illnesses, proximity to a school in a home country, political unrest, war, poverty, violence, and others. SLIFE often need support in building foundational skills in literacy and math. Older SLIFE need materials that aren't demeaning or baby-ish in appearance. Taking the necessary time to find age- and grade-appropriate materials is worthwhile to honor the integrity of older students with beginning levels of literacy skills.

### Students with Interrupted Programming in Their Education

SIPE (students with interrupted programming in their education) is a term that you may not have heard as much. Because school funding and multilingual program models are often based on local student populations, school districts—even those right next to each other—have different available programming options to their local student community. For example, in one district they may offer a one-way dual language program with a program goal of biliteracy. The district next door might only offer a Transitional Program Of Instruction (or TPI) with a program goal of literacy and proficiency in English. When a student moves once (or twice, or more) from one district to another, and their languaging and literacy journey is interrupted based on the program model, this is *interrupted programming*. This can impact a student's literacy journey and language journey.

### Former Multilinguals

Former multilinguals (or former ELs) are students who were once identified as a multilingual student, but they've reached "proficiency" according to their state's exit criteria on an annual language assessment. It is important to note that schools and districts are required to monitor former multilingual learners after exiting to ensure that they're able to continue to access grade-level content.

Even within each of these different student groups that exist underneath the large, diverse multilingual learner umbrella, each has their own language journey that marks their own individual histories and timelines—at what point(s) did they begin their multilingualism journey?

## Simultaneous vs. Sequential

The way we learn language typically falls into either *simultaneous multilingualism* or *sequential multilingualism*. Sequential multilingualism means that students first learn one language (through a combination of some domains or all domains of reading, writing, listening, and speaking), then start to learn and develop their additional language (also through a combination of some or all language domains). Sequential multilingualism is what we most often see with newcomer student populations, but of course, this is not always the case.

Simultaneous multilingualism is when students are learning, growing, and developing in two languages at the same time (also through a combination of some or all language domains). We often see students who are participating in a bilingual program or dual language program who are simultaneous multilinguals.

Knowing our students and their unique language journeys and experiences is critical as we advocate for equity.

## Question, Equip, Act

In this book, I will share the following framework of three prongs: *Question*, *Equip*, and *Act*. These three prongs have helped me to address my own knowledge, bias, misconceptions, misunderstandings. These have allowed me time and space to gather more information about myself and those around me. These have allowed me to move beyond mere acknowledgement of inequities. *Question*, *Equip*, and *Act* as a framework has built my own foundation in this work. Having such a structure has helped me to identify needs, develop a plan, and either push myself or my system forward in becoming more equitable for those I serve.

I'm going to prompt us to consider an example while using these three prongs. Let's imagine that Mari, the mother of a newcomer student, has expressed interest in connecting with other grownups (parents, guardians, and/or caregivers of students) recently at a parent-teacher conference where the EL teacher, 5th grade classroom teacher, social worker, and interpreter were present. Mari shared that she is starting English classes at the local community college, but her primary language is Lithuanian. The classroom teacher recommended that she join the PTA, but all their meetings are in English only. The EL teacher recommended joining the school's Bilingual Parent Advisory Council, and shared that she believes there's currently an interpreter who speaks Lithuanian who attends those meetings. Let's move through our three-prong process of Question, Equip, and Act with Mari's example.

**Question**—inquire about the world around you. Enter conversations from a genuinely inquisitive state of mind. Ask a lot of questions of yourself and others and ask again. Be genuinely, openly, and courageously curious in meetings, conversations with colleagues, and in dialogue with friends and family, as this will always help us all reflect and learn. People often say something along the lines of "there are no stupid questions." While this is true, learn how to ask great questions. Encourage others to ask great questions. Uproot deeper issues. Get to the root cause. Unlearn often—and this is much easier said than done, as unlearning requires humility when confronted with new information that may present you with uncomfortable truths about yourself or the world. Ask yourself about your beliefs, actions, and intentions. Be honest. Be humble. Be authentic. Keeping yourself open to new information (and revisiting old information) can help you reflect and serve from a place of reflection.

> When Mari first contacted the school, we had our own wonderings about what opportunities are currently available for her (and for other families as well) to connect with other grownups, so we gathered our list of questions for our team to investigate together. What groups or spaces does our school community already have that we know about? Which of these groups, if any, currently provide multilingual language access to grownups at their meetings or gatherings? Why do those groups have or not have multilingual language access? Whose responsibility is it to provide interpreters and/or translators? How might they secure these resources? Are there funds to support this? Are we required to provide this? Who oversees each of these groups? How does one join these groups or find information about these groups? When

and where do they meet? Do they offer any childcare or transportation to attend the meetings or gatherings? Is there a virtual option? How are each of these groups in terms of welcoming new members?

**Equip**—equip yourself with information regarding the historical, sociocultural, and political context within our specific scenarios. This includes a societal context, a local context, and a current context. Information can come in various forms. Information can come from history (including world history, education history, US history, and local history). Information includes facts and dates, but it also includes stories, perspectives, and lived experiences of all the folks within the school ecosystem: students, educators, change makers and allies, families, leaders, and community members. This also includes information about YOUR story (who you are, how you show up in spaces, why you show up in that way, how you came into your current space in education, and even why you picked up this book). Equipping yourself by gathering and collecting information about the world around you, your place in it, and how it all came to be how it is today will help you reflect and serve from a place of knowledge.

> We started to list out all of the different groups and spaces that we thought we'd share with Mari: We have the PTA, the sports booster club, our Bilingual Parent Advisory Council (BPAC), and our Local School Council. The classroom teacher and social worker on the team had never heard of the BPAC before, and the EL teacher shared that she never recommends the PTA to multilingual families because there hasn't historically been any language access. We learned that none of the groups currently have any linguistic access to users of other languages. Upon further digging, we found out that the Booster Club used to have a Korean-speaking parent, and they volunteered their bilingualism to interpret meetings for two other Korean-speaking families. However, their child graduated from our school system

three years ago, and so the group no longer has this as a resource. The new Sports Booster Club President noted that this year, there are no Korean-speaking (or Lithuanian-speaking) families, so according to them, "it's not really a need for our group." We learned that Mari's children do not plan to participate in sports this year, but they are interested in other activities. The PTA and the Local School Council have shared that they don't have any multilingual families in their groups so they "haven't had the need for interpreters or language access." The district's Bilingual Parent Advisory Council has had multiple interpreters over the years, across languages like Korean, Spanish, Ukrainian, Urdu, and Tagalog. This particular group is overseen by the multilingual department director, and she has arranged for interpreters for each of these meetings. This director has also had each of the invitations and flyers professionally translated and distributed to all multilingual families in the district via email, paper flyers sent directly to students, flyers posted in common areas inside and outside the school, and also shared on the district and the BPAC's social media pages. She has shared that they have several Lithuanian-speaking families who participate regularly, along with an interpreter.

The principal and multilingual director started to view the current membership lists of each of the groups and noted that there was very little engagement from multilingual families outside of the BPAC. They looked at each of the group's agendas and minutes, their calendars, their digital spaces, and their events. They sat down to interview a few monolingual families who participated in one or more groups, and also interviewed multilingual families who were active in BPAC as well as multilingual families who were not a part of any of these groups. Some multilingual families shared that they had never even heard of those groups. One multilingual mother interviewed expressed interest in the Booster Club because her son played football and soccer, and several folks indicated interest in joining the Local School Council.

**Act**—take action. Move the needle. Call yourself to action. Recognize the call to speak out, challenge others, make suggestions, learn, and take your system forward with you. What are the actions that you can take now? What are the next steps for you as an individual, next steps for your team, next steps for leadership, and next steps for your school, your district, and/or your system? Be super specific with outcomes. Establish checkpoints and a calendar of dates to revisit and check progress. Moving yourself and your learning forward requires you to take risks and make mistakes. You will rub people the wrong way. You will ruffle feathers. You will lose friends. You will lose the respect of others, and you will lose respect for other people. While uncomfortable and difficult, this is part of the process. Acknowledge, appreciate, and celebrate the "small wins" but don't settle for them.

> We noted that we needed to build better awareness amongst staff of the various groups and spaces we have to support families, so we asked the district communications director to put together a one-pager that has the name of each group, a contact person, the group's purpose, and the dates of their fall meetings. Our principal was going to put this into our next staff newsletter. We found it troubling that only the EL teacher knew about the district's BPAC. The classroom teacher expressed discomfort in not knowing about this group, "Is this new?! I could've been recommending this group to families at our Back to School Night for the past 12 years I've been here!" Our multilingual director said she would secure translations of this one-pager in multiple languages so that they can also be distributed to families, and the classroom teacher said she will give this to Mari next week when she chaperones for the field trip.
>
> The multilingual director reviewed with our team about when translations and interpretations were

required in order to be in compliance with the law, and she also shared some additional recommended best practices. They set a date on the calendar to review these requirements and best practices with the rest of the staff at our next meeting.

The multilingual director and principal decided that they needed to present information to each of these groups' leadership teams about being linguistically inclusive to all families. It is possible that school staff and leadership may never have had this conversation with each of these groups or their leaders before. We guessed that these groups may not have understood the needs of the entire school community beyond their current membership. After meeting with each group's leadership teams, most were responsive and were willing to try a few new strategies to engage all families. The PTA was especially excited to try a new technology feature to translate their social media posts into multiple languages.

The new president of the Booster Club said that since Mari does not plan on participating this year, they "don't have to worry about doing any of that stuff." After the multilingual director shared our district's commitment to being inclusive to all families, the president doubled down and said that he didn't have time for all of that, and that shouldn't be his responsibility or the responsibility of his group, because he's monolingual and all of the current members of the group are monolingual. When the principal suggested that perhaps multilingual families haven't participated in the group since the Korean-speaking family left, the president responded that he's just volunteering his valuable time and he's not getting paid for any of this. He went on to say that if he continues to be "harassed about all this equity crap," he will go to the superintendent and the school board. The principal went quiet (he doesn't always get along with two of the school board members), but the multilingual director asked if he needed the superintendent's contact information.

After the meeting, the multilingual director contacted the superintendent and asked to collaboratively develop a presentation that they could deliver to the board.

## Question, Equip, and Act as a Process

Through the above description and example, we can see how powerful the process of Question, Equip, and Act can be in order to make a profound impact in educational spaces.

To have just one of these components missing could derail our work. If we don't take the time to be courageously curious and ask questions (Question), we may be missing out on important details and perspectives. If we fail to empower ourselves with information about current realities, broad or local history, or explore the lived experiences of those we serve and support (Equip), we cannot adequately address any needed changes. If we fail to take action on any of the inequities that we uncover (Act), we are creating systems that will continue to abdicate responsibility of real equity for multilingual learners.

This process allows us to be reflective as individuals and also invite others into the work as we go. Question, Equip, and Act can serve as a framework for us and our systems to work through specific scenarios of inequities that impact multilingual learners and families that we encounter as educators and leaders.

## Moving Beyond Entry Points

Equity and advocacy for multilingual learners goes beyond simply acknowledging that we have linguistic diversity—although this might be a very valid entry point and invitation to the work. It goes beyond celebrating linguistic diversity—which again, can be a very valid entry point and invitation to the work. I don't mind entry points. In fact, I think sometimes that this can be the impetus to having larger scale transformations. However, there is also great danger in entry points, because sometimes this is where people stop their work. "Yay! I used Ukrainian subtitles in the YouTube video to help my students! Now my lesson is completely accessible!" or "Woohoo! I made a multilingual poster for this math unit! I honored linguistic diversity in this unit!" Some folks may find satisfaction in the general acknowledgement or that initial step, and fail to push beyond that. What else? What's next?

 **Let's Go!**

As we dive into this work, you may be uncomfortable or challenged in a practice, and I invite you to lean into the discomfort. Allow yourself to feel it and process it. Also identify those action steps for you as an individual or for your system.

Below is an example of the Question, Equip, Act framework that will be at the end of each chapter. I'd encourage you to find a space to capture your thinking for each of these prompts.

You already got this far. Let's go! Let's Ignite Real Change!

**TABLE 1.2** Question, Equip, Act (Chapter 1)

| Question | Equip | Act |
|---|---|---|
| Who are the students I serve? What do I know about them? What do I not yet know about them? | Consider the ways you gather information about students and families you serve. Ask colleagues how they gather information. | Explore your multilingual learner population. Aside from what languages are present, what else do you know about their unique language stories and journeys? |
| Who are the families I serve? | | Ask your colleagues to reflect on who/ what shaped their languaging journey. Most monolingual folks have never been asked this question! |
| Why did I pick up this book? What are my hopes and intentions for reading this? | Define equity. Ask your colleagues to define equity. List examples and non-examples. | |

*(Continued)*

**TABLE 1.2** (Continued)

| Question | Equip | Act |
|---|---|---|
| What are some inequities that I already recognize within my own system? | Define advocacy. List characteristics of advocates. Capture things they might say or do. | Compile a list of Green Flags you've seen or experienced in your system lately. |
| Does my current district think that "equity" is a bad word? Why? | Write down your role/title in your system. List your responsibilities as it relates to equity for multilingual students. Be specific. No matter your role, you have responsibilities in this area! | Compile a list of Red Flags you've seen or experienced in your system lately. Choose one Red Flag to share with a trusted colleague. What might be one potential next step for you? |
| What are the perceptions of multilingual students in your school? | | Turn the page! Keep reading! |

# 2
# Cultivating Multilingual Mindsets Across a School Community

I have two dogs in my home—a Shih Tzu that does not shed and a Great Dane mix that definitely sheds. We have parts of our home that are carpeted, and I've always had a thing about excessively vacuuming the carpets ever since my kids were born (going on 17-ish years ago). While I can be diligent about the amount of times I vacuum each week (or even each day), there are teeny, tiny strands of dog hair that fall in between the threads of carpeting that seem to embed themselves in and hold on tight for dear life when the vacuum gets rolling. I can vacuum the carpet over and over, and that dog hair stays. To the naked eye, after stepping back, I can admire the clean vacuum lines and appreciate how clean the carpet now appears to be. To the eye that looks a little closer, there's still tons of dog hair. Ew. I purchased one of those carpet cleaning tools that resemble a rake after seeing countless ads online. I was excited to give it a whirl, knowing I have one shedding dog. After vacuuming like I normally do, I pulled the tool out of the box and began to scrape the carpet. What came up was horrifying. In no less than 20 minutes, I had slowly acquired a furball of Great Dane hair that could be compared to the size of the Shih Tzu. Gross!

This is similar to going deeper in our schools—in our conversations, in our decision making, in our thoughts and mindsets, and in our actions. If we have dog hair tangled into the fibers of the carpet and we're content with just vacuuming, we're not going to get very far. If we have linguistically oppressive mindsets that influence our practices, and we're okay with just "celebrating language" sometimes at an International Night, then our systems won't experience transformational change. Our efforts will remain surface-level.

In order to advocate for the students, families, and communities we serve, we must get really honest about current rhetoric that flows through discourse and dialogue inside and outside of our schools. First, it's important that we are connected to all the different folks across the school ecosystem—this includes students, teachers, leaders, families, board members, and other community members. When we have connected relationships, we can better tap into the feelings and the current understandings that exist, ebb, and flow throughout the fibers of the school. It's important that we can nurture and sustain those relationships to allow for open dialogue. When others feel comfortable opening up to us, we can better understand various points of view and diversity of thought. When we can establish and then nurture open lines of communication, we can better serve as connectors and allow for honest conversations to unfold, free of judgment, with an open eye to potential entry points into honest and brave dialogue.

While yes, we absolutely exist in a multilingual world, we have to acknowledge the historical linguistic oppression that has run rampant in the US, and how this has been intricately linked to anti-immigrant rhetoric.

## Addressing Anti-Immigrant Rhetoric

In our most recent presidential election in 2024, there were candidates who admitted to inventing stories that led to physical and emotional harm to Haitian immigrants. The candidates' stories incited violence against an entire immigrant community (of tens of thousands of human beings, including children). Schools, libraries, and hospitals had to be shut down due to bomb threats and other threats of violence because of the fabricated stories shared by these politicians and repeated by their supporters. This led to widespread fear amongst the Haitian immigrant community, not only in that particular region, but across the country.

To ignore that this is a current reality of our students and families and taking no action to address this head-on is educational malpractice. We have to denounce, at every turn, any hate-fueled anti-immigrant words, messaging, rhetoric, memes, pictures, social media posts—it all must be denounced. Every time.

How might we grapple with this internally as a staff serving a linguistically and culturally rich community? One potential step might be for individual educators and leaders to broaden our understanding and perspectives by following organizations on social media that bring these issues to the forefront, such as the American Civil Liberties Union (ACLU), the National Immigrant Justice Center, United We Dream, The Young Center for Immigrant Children's Rights, and Immigrant Connections, just to name a few. Another potential small step might be to share an article or blog post with colleagues and teammates about the impact of anti-immigrant rhetoric and have a dedicated time and space to read, discuss, and plan together.

One very necessary small step would be to come together as teammates and discuss language to use when confronted with anti-immigrant rhetoric inside of the classroom, with colleagues, with leaders, or with community members. Statements like, "I disagree with what you said," or "We do not accept or tolerate hate speech here," can sometimes feel simplistic for some, but I can attest that during moments where I've heard harmful statements inside of schools, my heart drops and my brain feels like it screeches to a halt. I can't think straight. Practicing these statements regularly and having them mentally ready can help us feel more prepared if and when we're ever confronted with moments of harm.

Externally, how your school and district chooses to address these moments shows your students and families a lot. It shows your immigrant community what you stand for and what you allow. It also shows your privileged groups the same thing. Your school or district's silence during these times can also feel deafening. It tells your immigrant community how little you care—do you even acknowledge the existence of dangerous rhetoric?

How can we do this in a way that demonstrates an inclusive community where all deserve to feel safe? I observed a district where, in response to these situations, the superintendent wrote a letter to community members that was concise but clearly articulated a commitment to ensuring the emotional and physical safety and well-being of all students and families. It was only a paragraph long but the message was easy to understand—that all students deserve to feel safe at school.

I also watched a few districts which, in response to these situations, created videos for their social media accounts. One such video showed various staff members in various school settings (the cafeteria, several classrooms, hallways, and the front office) sharing the same message, "Here at ___ School, we all belong." Another such video featured students who shared their favorite parts of school, and at the end of the video the students said, "I deserve to feel safe and happy at my school!"

Another school district posted a series of activities that students were doing across their instructional days to express their fears, worries, and realities. Some of these included writing prompts, decompression activities, reading specific and relevant picture books, and creating art. Some students made posters for common areas in the hallways that had student sentiments like, "My mom is important to me," and "I will stand up for myself and others," and "Words can hurt." The district shared in their posts that the world can feel scary and heavy but that at school, we all deserve to feel safe to express ourselves, share our worries, and take action in ways that feel good to us.

Another district shared a letter from a principal that acknowledged the fears, worries, and anxieties that were being experienced by students, families, and community members. The school didn't pretend to have all the answers, but there was communication that this was difficult to grapple with and that all the staff are continuing to have ongoing conversations about potential actions that they could explore together. The letter also shared resources for students and adults in the school community. Finally, the letter invited families to share their thoughts and feelings with the school, so that collectively they could build bridges.

Regardless of your own political views and beliefs, and the views and beliefs of political candidates you choose to support, we can and should all remain open to understanding the cause and also the effect of harmful rhetoric.

Anti-immigrant rhetoric is dangerous in and of itself, and while the "louder" moments are easier for us to spot, it's also baked into our schools' carpets. To understand this fully, let's examine just some of the historical legislation that has impacted multilingual students.

### Mendez vs. Westminster

In Mendez vs. Westminster (1946), the family of Sylvia Mendez, an eight-year-old girl, won a class action lawsuit against four school districts in California for the public school segregation of Mexican students, after Sylvia was denied entry to a "white" school. This case eventually led the entire state of California to outlaw segregation in its schools, which made them the first state to desegregate their public schools. About eight years later, the US Supreme Court ruled in the case of Brown vs. Board of Education that racial segregation in schools was unconstitutional.

Build awareness of this story and this court case by exploring the beautiful picture book, *Separate Is Never Equal: Sylvia Mendez and Her Family's Fight for Desegregation*, written and illustrated by Duncan Tonatiuh.

### Lau vs. Nichols

In the case of Lau vs. Nichols (1974), 1,800 Chinese students and families, including the family of nine-year-old Kinney Kimmon Lau, sued the San Francisco Unified School District for not providing English instruction to students whose heritage language was Chinese. This Supreme Court case references and upholds the Civil Rights Act of 1964, due to educational discrimination. This case is often referenced by multilingual education advocates and educators who work to ensure that all students have access to high-quality language acquisition and language development programs and opportunities.

## Plyler vs. Doe

Plyler vs. Doe (1982) was a landmark Supreme Court case that states that it is unconstitutional to deny public education to immigrant students. What does this mean? It means that there were entire school systems across the country already denying students—children—of these basic rights. It also means that they had to create a law to protect students—children—of these basic rights. This case occurred in 1982, which means that there are still human beings in our country and, more specifically, at our decision-making tables in schools who still question whether or not we should provide an education to immigrant children. Before you tell me that this seems outlandish and far-fetched, let's address the tiptoe. Yes, folks retire. *And also—* folks mentor younger generations of educators, principals, school board members, policy-makers, etc. Our practices and beliefs that we pass down often go unchecked under the guise of "this is tradition" an "this is how we make decisions here" and "this is how we do things." It's important to note that anti-immigrant rhetoric still runs pervasively through every institution of the US.

Reflect with students and staff by exploring the beautiful picture book titled *Free to Learn: How Alfredo Lopez Fought for the Right to Go to School* by Cynthia Levinson and illustrated by Mirelle Ortega.

## Seeking Out Historical Context

In a time where it's considered controversial whether or not to teach accurate history, it is critical that as educators and leaders, we are informed of where our schools have been, especially as it relates to serving and supporting multilingual students and their families. To deny history is to deny reality. We have to understand historical and political context so that we can serve as better advocates and lead for real change in our schools.

Considering how and when (and from who and where) we seek out historical context also matters. Our schools' textbooks in the US have been notorious for their ability to whitewash history, meaning they've prioritized the white experience, have only listened to white voices and perspectives, and have only provided sentiments and messages that are comfortable and digestible to a white audience. There are many examples of this, such as the teaching of "The First Thanksgiving" being a cutesy story of Pilgrims and Indigenous Peoples coming together around a meal, without discussion or acknowledgement of colonization, stolen land, or the murder of indigenous peoples. Just curious, reader. What is YOUR positionality and what were YOU taught about "The First Thanksgiving," and who taught it to you?

I can speak to my own lived experiences as a white girl who was taught by white teachers and raised by white parents. I was absolutely taught the cutesy story at school. My mom pushed our perspectives at home when my sisters and I were kids, and she helped us to understand that real history was a lot more difficult to stomach. She shared with us that telling the truth about history might be harder for some folks, like white teachers or white textbook writers, because confronting a history that doesn't paint us white folks nicely can feel uncomfortable. My mom taught us that confronting the ugly parts of history are necessary for all of us, especially for those of us with certain privileges.

I remember once coming home from school and telling my mom that Abraham Lincoln was SUCH a hero because he "ended slavery." *Wow, Mom! How fantastic! What a great man! Racism ended that day!* Umm, ew. Not quite. Remember my lived experience as a white girl who was taught by white teachers who used textbooks written by—yes, more white folks. So those words I was sharing were my understanding of what I was taught. She questioned why I was learning about another way to praise another white man. She also went a little deeper with me about Abraham Lincoln. She encouraged me to consider how US slavery still impacted life today.

Later in elementary school, I remember learning about Dr. Martin Luther King, Jr. We listened to his speech at school and I was sure my mom would be happy that we weren't learning about yet another white dude. I came home to report what I learned and I said, "Isn't it great that he got rid of racism?" She explained that his courage helped teach the world and reshape the country, but that racism wasn't gone. Civil rights are still things that many folks continue to fight for each day (and goodness, we still have these very same conversations decades later). She read my sisters and I "The Letter from a Birmingham Jail." Later she took us to the theatre to watch Denzel Washington play Malcolm X. She showed us newspaper pictures from the library. She wanted us to have a deeper understanding of the Civil Rights Movement, beyond what our school was teaching us.

As a white mom raising white kids, I've had my eyes and ears open to what they've been taught in their schools as it relates to history, and whose voices, experiences, and perspectives have been prioritized, and whose voices, experiences, and perspectives are ignored, briefly mentioned, or "represented" by a white voice. I want them to understand how that shapes our understanding. I feel like this is my responsibility as a white mom raising white kids.

Understanding history and unpacking the storytelling and messaging is critical to being a better advocate. It is critical to advocating for equity for multilingual students and families.

## Positioning Grit and Resilience

We need to move away from praising our students' and families' grit and resilience and instead address the inequities that require their grit and resilience. No student or family should have to rise above an inequitable system. Rising above and succeeding in the face of inequity shouldn't be the expectation of our students and families. It certainly shouldn't be the goal of education.

This position of praising grit and resilience has roots in the old "bootstrap" mentality of the olden days. I say olden days here because this is where that mentality should have stayed. Perhaps you've heard the saying, "Folks should pull themselves up by their bootstraps" to express a sentiment of immigrants making their own way without seeking support. Did you happen to know that this saying was actually always said sarcastically because it's literally impossible to pull yourself up physically by your bootstraps? Go ahead. Try on some boots and try it out. Impossible! Anyway, the phrase was just used so much over years and across generations that now it exists as a phrase that has been weaponized by folks in power to insinuate that entire populations of immigrants should have to navigate life independently with GRIT and RESILIENCE in order to pursue some sort of "American Dream" ideal.

One common example of this in classrooms is when teachers or leaders express the idea that kids (or their families) must learn English right away and it should be "on them" (or on their families) to figure it out "because my grandparents did it." Someone specifically said to me "my grandparents had to figure that out—so these kids need to do it, too." I feel like that statement completely misses the point—shouldn't we wish for educational systems to be supportive of everyone? I personally wish my great-grandparents had more access to support back then, rather than saying, "it was hard for them so therefore it should be hard for everyone."

Non-indigenous people in the US will try to make the erroneous comparison between their ancestor's immigration stories with the immigration stories of today, even though the political climate, rhetoric, laws, circumstances, and access to resources may be wildly different. "But my great-grandparents did it." You're right—they did—AND we can also recognize that today's immigration stories, systems, and structures are not the same as those of the past. This is not to negate any difficulties that our families have experienced in their immigration stories. I know that my own great-grandmother who came on a ship from Hungary and eventually made her way to Chicago had plenty of difficulties. I cannot even imagine what she went through. No doubt there were significant challenges that she faced! I can acknowledge that AND ALSO acknowledge that today's experience is different.

## Linguistic Oppression

What is linguistic oppression? This refers to the harm caused (whether or not it was "intended") by the words or actions that positions others' languaging as inferior or less than. This happens across and within languages by those with more linguistic power. Linguistic oppression occurs both explicitly and implicitly.

## Explicit Linguistic Oppression

I have to express immense gratitude for the work of Dr. José Medina, who has taught me a lot about linguistic oppression. Through his work and even through his social media posts, he presents different thoughts, ideas, examples, and considerations for linguistically oppressive practices in our schools and communities. I have learned so much from him, and I've become more and more aware of linguistic oppression.

When I speak with schools, I often share a children's book published by Sesame Street in 2022 called *Spanish is My SuperPower*. It shows one of the Sesame Street characters, Rosita, recounting an event that occurred at a supermarket while she was shopping with her mom. She explains to her friends that she and her mom were approached by someone in the store who told them, "Excuse me, but we speak only English here. We don't speak Spanish" (Correa et al., 2022). Each time I share this part of the text, I feel angry all over again. For me, this book is powerful for a number of reasons. It shows the disgusting reality that many of our students and families face. I use the term "disgusting" very intentionally here. It is disgusting that families who are languaging with each other while out in the community in their heritage language are being silenced, challenged, harassed, or intimidated. This isn't okay. Another reason that this book is so powerful is because it gives families, educators, and grownups some context to have these discussions with students and to help them remember that other people's ignorance does not take away from their gift of bilingualism. Finally, this book is so impactful because it is a call to action. Yes, this is designed for our youngest learners. Remember that Sesame Street's target audience is early childhood, along with the grownups who care for young children. The fact that Sesame Street had to design a resource to help our youngest learners navigate linguistic oppression in their communities (in 2022, no less) calls us all in and tells us that we have work to do.

Human beings in communities across the US have experienced discrimination, hate, and physical and/or emotional violence when utilizing a language other than English. These attacks happen in supermarkets, parking lots, sports stadiums, post offices, public libraries, and more. They also happen at family gatherings, social events, and in the workplace. This means that our students and families have likely experienced these moments in their lives—at all ages. As our students enter our classrooms, how do we reckon with this?

Unfortunately, as I mentioned earlier—this also happens inside the school. As we discussed in Chapter 1, *the call is coming*

**FIGURE 2.1** An example of two books that demonstrate linguistic oppression, and later linguistic empowerment.
Photograph by the author.

*from inside the building!* Let's explore a few moments of linguistic oppression inside our schools.

When a decision-making matrix denies a student access to gifted/enrichment or advanced placement courses and opportunities because of their level of English language proficiency, this is linguistic oppression.

When a district official sends home vital communication regarding student safety in English only, this is linguistic oppression.

When a district employee tells students in the cafeteria, "Don't speak Spanish! Speak English—it's the only way to learn!" This is linguistic oppression.

Are your linguistic oppression lenses on fire yet?

Just as dangerous as explicit acts of linguistic oppression, it's often the implicit attacks on languaging that have existed in the air that have gone undetected, unnoticed, and unaddressed by those with privilege and power that continue to cause harm to those we serve.

## Implicit Linguistic Oppression

We have to acknowledge and continue to uproot and disrupt the *implicit* practices, actions, and beliefs. These might be harder for us to identify. These can also be more difficult for some to connect to linguistic oppression—but let's name it. Call it what it is. Let's explore some examples.

When a school district member either explicitly tells or even insinuates to a family member or caregiver of a student that speaking more than one language is confusing for a child, this is linguistic oppression.

When a speech pathologist or audiologist tells the grownup of a child that they should only focus on teaching their child one language, this is linguistic oppression.

When a teacher tells a student that they should stop reading books in Mongolian and just focus on reading in English because it'll help them learn better, this is linguistic oppression.

Your senses may be ignited now!

## Walking, Breathing Linguistic Oppression

You might be thinking "Hey Carly, I totally see what you're saying but my school isn't like that. We don't have linguistically oppressive practices." Cool. Let's review a few scenarios that happen in a lot of schools and classrooms and then you can let me know if you still think your school doesn't have linguistically oppressive practices (spoiler alert—all of these are linguistically oppressive practices).

> Scenario 1: A teacher puts up a sign in a classroom of monolingual and multilingual learners that says "No Spanish."
>
> Scenario 2: A teacher puts up a sign in a classroom of monolingual and multilingual learners that has a "word graveyard" and/or a "banned word list" with AAVE, slang, and/or other specific language choices utilized by historically minoritized groups.
>
> Scenario 3: A teacher told a colleague privately that their accent is "so cute/cool/adorable."
>
> Scenario 4: A teacher told a colleague in front of students that their accent is "so cute/cool/adorable."
>
> Scenario 5: A principal told a colleague privately, or in front of colleagues, or in front of students, that their accent is "so cute/cool/adorable."
>
> Scenario 6: The teachers in the building send home newsletters in English and no other languages. OR The district communications director sent out a time-sensitive safety advisory message in English and no other languages.
>
> Scenario 7: An adult at school asks a student who shares a language with a newcomer student to translate for them for the next few days in math, science, social studies, language arts, art, PE, and also requests that they sit together in the cafeteria and also that they hang out together during recess.

> Scenario 8: An interventionist counted a mispronounced proper noun on a standardized reading fluency assessment as an error.
>
> Scenario 9: A monolingual student asks another student why we have so many "Spanish kids" in a classroom at school (special note for more context—in this case, the child was referring to Spanish languagers, as not one child was from Spain).
>
> Scenario 10: A principal asks the bilingual classroom teacher to "just really quickly translate" this 30 page document over the weekend (because if she doesn't do it, we won't have it available for our Spanish-speaking families!).

How do these scenarios demonstrate linguistic oppression? Are there one or more of these where you're struggling to locate the oppression? Have you yourself experienced these or similar scenarios?

Let's continue.

Linguistic oppression isn't just present in these scenarios. It's also heavily baked into our instructional practices and grading practices as well. Writing is a real doozy of a topic when we talk about linguistic oppression.

## Linguistic Superiority

Linguistic superiority is also something that we must recognize in schools. We've seen plenty of examples of this on social media. In the comments section of any public post on Facebook or other social media platforms, strangers will discuss issues in the comments and take a side. Inevitably, someone will start an argument about whatever the post is about. When the strangers run out of content or have exhausted their stance, they'll resort to correcting each other's languaging (you name it—spelling, grammar, vocabulary choice—it's all there). Linguistic superiority isn't just reserved for online forums though—we also see it in various moments in our schools.

All of us have been taught both explicitly and implicitly what "good writing" looks like and sounds like. When it comes down to it, in schools (from elementary up through high school, at the university level and especially in academia), "good writing" centers whiteness. Within schools, linguistic superiority often presents itself by demanding students to speak, write, or express themselves in a particular way.

Now, reader, you may struggle reading this very book with how I write. How I use my voice. How I might start a sentence "incorrectly." Or how I'll sometimes just use phrases instead of an "actual, complete" sentence. Perhaps you'll grow frustrated with how I move in and out of my social and academic registers throughout this book. Perhaps you will judge my languaging and writing style in an effort to determine if the way I express myself is "academic enough" to be taken seriously.

I've been told to ditch my informal registers when speaking or delivering a major keynote to a district because "people will not take you seriously." Cool. Don't take me seriously then. Sounds like a YOU problem. I also wear "too much pink" and truly, I worry for your worry, but that's a whole different conversation.

In a world where linguistic oppression continues to run rampant and worsens with each political election, let's keep our feelers up and out. Becoming better at identifying and naming linguistically oppressive practices is a key part to this work. You might run across a scenario in your work where a situation rubs you the wrong way and you can't quite put your finger on exactly what or why. Having someone process this moment with you can sometimes help. Sometimes we ask ourselves, "is this an example of linguistic oppression or am I reading too deeply into this?" Well. If it looks like a duck, and sounds like a duck . . . it's probably linguistic oppression. Name it. Call it how it feels. Call it what it is.

Also—don't let others gaslight you into thinking that you're reading too far into a situation. You're not. Sometimes that "assume positive intent" crap really causes a whole lot of damage. It gaslights us into thinking we should just "consider another perspective" or "assume the best in someone" even when they say something especially harmful, racist, or oppressive. Friend, you don't have to assume any positive intent. Instead, address the impact.

Positive intent can kiss my you-know-what, sometimes. You know?

## Positioning Multilingualism

> ### Voices from the Field
>
> ***Valerie Peña Hernández, Strategic Advisor for K-12 Curriculum and Instruction (Multilingual and Special Education Specialization)***
>
> As someone who has worked across the nation, from rural America to international schools, I've seen that many other countries celebrate bilingualism and prioritize teaching children two languages at once. In contrast, America often focuses on promoting the language of power—English—a dangerous concept that assumes other languages are less important. Until we recognize that being a global citizen holds more value than forcing someone to abandon their identity to fit a mold, we cannot truly embrace the whole child. As an educator who has worked with diverse student populations, I firmly believe that embracing and celebrating multilingualism is crucial for creating an inclusive and equitable learning environment. It is essential to recognize the value of every language and culture represented in our schools. We must move away from the notion that English is the sole language of power and create spaces where all languages are celebrated and

> respected. By doing so, we empower our students to embrace their identities and foster a sense of belonging in the school community.

Let's have an honest rundown of how we position multilingualism in our spaces. While it's wonderful to think about celebrating multilingualism, there is a nuance here that we need to be mindful of in this work.

### Centering White Bilingualism

When we praise white bilingualism and reject heritage bilingualism, that's a problem. Let me give you an example. As a white teacher who has served multilingual learners, I have had this happen a good handful of times, especially early on in my career. Upon meeting someone new who looks like me and sounds like me, they'd discover that I was the "EL teacher," and they'd ask "Ohhh so do you speak a lot of languages?" *Sidenote here—it's actually not a job requirement. Who'da thunk?* Anyway, I'd respond that I can speak English and Spanish. This would almost always elicit the response of, "Wowww Carlyyyyy! That's soooo cool that you're bilingual!!!! How amazinggg!" and sometimes there'd be a mini follow-up connection about their study abroad experience once in college. Literally moments later (or sure—sometimes days later), they'd point out a multilingual student in my class (or their class) and say, "They're so low-performing because they have a language barrier."

Umm. What?!

Here comes my dad—"THROW THE FLAG!" Yes, Dad. Indeed.

When my white bilingualism is praised while students' or families' heritage bilingualism is slandered, this is one example of living, breathing linguistic oppression. We can't say that we "value languages," that we "appreciate linguistic diversity," or that we recognize the linguistic identities of students and families we serve in these moments.

## Positioning Languages as Barriers

We've grown so accustomed to referring to languages as barriers. Have you noticed that? We've positioned languages as barriers. As problems. As a hurdle. As an obstacle. Something that must be overcome. A problem that must be solved. Something that must be fixed.

My entire life I've heard the phrase "language barrier," and it has started to make me itchier and itchier over the years the more I hear it. Our intentions of using that phrase are also important to note, but not always easy to recognize or identify. Many times, we are referring to the inability for us to communicate or connect with a student or family that we serve because we don't have a shared language with which to do so. However, when any one of us routinely positions language as a barrier, it can lead to problematic mindsets and beliefs about our language identities.

We should reflect on identifying WHO possesses the barrier. I most often overhear and experience the "barrier" being held by a student or family who doesn't possess English languaging skills at that moment (as in, "I can't call home because they have a language barrier"). I very infrequently overhear and experience English languagers claiming that barrier (as in, "I am having trouble calling home because I have a language barrier"). The positioning is important here, especially as we unpack power and privilege behind English languagers, and linguistic oppression of speakers of other languages in US schools.

Languages are not barriers to overcome. Languages are pieces of who we are. They are pieces of our identities. They are elements of our cultures—how we read, write, listen, speak, view, represent, interpret, recount, describe, storytell, question, and more. Our languages and our languaging help shape how we see the world around us. Languages help us to connect and engage with each other. How could we possibly see them as a problem? Many times we refer to barriers as something we must break. Our languages are not in need of breaking.

*Okay, Carly. You're getting a little wrapped up in language policing here. If I can't say "language barrier," what should I say?*

Thanks for bringing us back to reflective language usage! Let's consider our intention for what we're trying to express here. If I'm trying to indicate that the other party I'm trying to communicate with doesn't have a shared language, I can express that: "We don't have a shared language." If I'm trying to indicate that we have a need for language access, I can express that: "Because we don't have a shared language, I'll request an interpreter." See? It's easier than we might've thought.

### Repositioning Multilingualism

In an effort to position multilingualism as a positive thing, organizations have often shared data points or research studies about the benefits of being multilingual. Folks are excited to share that being multilingual can reduce an individual's chance of developing dementia later in life. Folks are happy to report that multilingual people are more cognitively flexible.

Additionally, folks will excitedly share about the economic benefits of being multilingual. I've heard countless adults tell students (and in full transparency—I've done this as well) that being multilingual will open the doors to more possibilities in the future! Yay! You might even make more money because you can speak more than one language! You might be able to have an advantage some day in getting a job! Super!

I've told students many times over the years that the more languages you know, the more people you can help. We can help strangers at the grocery store and at the airport. We truly can serve as language liaisons everywhere we go! Woohoo!

The problem with all of this is that when we praise "benefits," we ignore the identity piece of languaging. Because our languages are tied to our identities, our families, and our cultures, it is harmful to constantly overemphasize how beneficial someone's identity is TO OTHERS. Our languages are inherently valuable all on their own. Let's de-emphasize how one's identity can benefit others and instead emphasize how one's identity is ALREADY valuable. It's valuable to ourselves. It's valuable to our family. It's valuable. Period.

## Seal of Biliteracy

In 2008, the group Californians Together began work in developing the Seal of Biliteracy. Today, all 50 states and Washington, DC implement The Seal of Biliteracy This is a prestigious award that can be given to students who demonstrate a high level of biliteracy. This can be given by a school, district, or regional office of education. Schools and districts across the country demonstrate various celebrations of this honor for their students. Some distribute a special cord that awardees can wear for graduation commencement ceremonies, and others celebrate this achievement with a certificate or medal presented to students. This movement is powerful in demonstrating how communities can honor an incredible achievement.

When we unpack who in our systems (at either our local level, our regional level, or state level) are the recipients of The Seal of Biliteracy, we must examine this data with a critical eye. Many students who participate in bilingual programs (including dual language programs) may eventually become eligible for this honor. When we uncover and confront the gentrification of two-way dual language programs, we see that we systematically prioritize the bilingualism, performance, and achievement of the white students. If the heritage English languagers are obtaining the Seal of Biliteracy with more frequency than the heritage languagers of the additional language, then this is a . . . (wait for it. . .) RED FLAG. Yep, you got it! This must act as not only a moment of reflection but a call to action.

## Identifying the Work at the Classroom Level

There are specific actions that we can take within our classrooms, whether or not we are multilingual, to elevate the presence of languages other than English in our spaces.

Within our own classrooms, we can conduct Language Inventories to analyze the visible language presence of our physical spaces.

We can incorporate our community languages by maintaining and dedicating spaces for multilingual presence on the physical walls and digital walls of our learning spaces. We can also create dedicated time and opportunities to actively invite students to converse in the language of their choice, either independently or with each other. This can be done easily within our partner or group structures, student recordings, independent writing, and more. See Table 2.1 for some initial ideas.

If you yourself utilize another language, model how you incorporate that in your think-alouds, read-alouds, and write-alouds. If you have a colleague who shares your additional language, engage with them in your languages so that students and colleagues can see examples of how adults utilize their full language skillset for both educational learning purposes and also social exchanges.

Within our classrooms, we should have audible and physical evidence that other languages not only exist, but that they're actively encouraged. Our languages should be heard in the air from students and adults in the classroom. Our languages should be seen easily (without searching) through written expressions on the walls, inside of notebooks, in anchor charts, on multilingual word walls, in our inspirational posters, and in our instructional materials.

**TABLE 2.1** Five Things to Say to Students to Invite Languages into the Classroom

| Five Things to Say to Students to Invite Languages into the Classroom |
|---|
| "As you work in groups today, please use the language of your choice." |
| "During independent writing, feel free to get your thoughts captured in English, Mongolian, or a combination of your languages." |
| "As you partner with each other, feel free to use your technology to help you share ideas across languages." |
| "As we express our learning today, use your full linguistic toolkit! Some words, phrases, and sentences may flow between languages, and that's awesome." |
| "Before we write today, if you want to record some initial thoughts in an audio, feel free to speak in English and French to get your first thoughts captured." |

## Identifying the Work at a School or District Level

Examine your common areas of the school, including hallways, bathrooms, gymnasiums, and cafeterias. Also pay attention to the common offices that all students have frequent access to, including the front office, principal's office, social worker's office, and the nurse's office. Analyze what's on the walls of those spaces. You might wish to conduct a Language Inventory of these spaces. This can be done by individual teachers or a team of colleagues. You may also wish to invite students into the process by having them analyze the language presence of the school and present their findings to teachers. After initial findings are shared, collaboratively design a goal, and set a date on your calendar to check progress.

## Exploring Multilingual Mindsets Through Picture Books

At both the classroom and school (or even district) levels, we can utilize tools like picture books to support this work. There is a large collection of picture books that can help us to facilitate conversations (and eventually, actions) about multilingual mindsets, understandings, and perspectives. Some of these demonstrate linguistic oppression while others demonstrate examples of linguistic elevation. These may be books that we utilize as we engage with this work at various stages—whether we are trying to engage a colleague in initial conversations or make wide-scale changes within our systems. See Table 2.2 for some examples of picture books.

**TABLE 2.2** Books that Highlight Multilingual Mindsets

| Book Title | Author |
|---|---|
| How to Speak in Spanglish | Monica Mancillas |
| Spanish Is the Language of My Family | Michael Genhart; John Parra |
| Spanish Is My SuperPower! | Maria Correa |
| ¡El español es mi superpoder! | Maria Correa |
| Gibberish | Young Vo |
| The Rock in my Throat | Kao Kalia Yang |
| When We Were Alone | David A. Robertson |

## Let's Go!

As we examine our own mindsets, and the mindsets of our systems, we can start to Question, Equip, and Act to move our schools forward. It begins with addressing our histories and recognizing the contexts that contribute to our mindsets. Now, let's get ready to affirm and honor the linguistic identities of those we serve.

Let's go! Let's Ignite Real Change!

**TABLE 2.3** Question, Equip, Act (Chapter 2)

| Question | Equip | Act |
| --- | --- | --- |
| In my upbringing, what perspectives have been prioritized when I was taught history? Why was that? | Identify your curricular resources and analyze the voices and perspectives that are represented. | Identify an equity checkpoint or even a considerations guide for any district or school team that explores new potential curricular resources. |
| In our curricular resources, whose voices and experiences are prioritized or centered? Why is that? | Research federal and state laws that protect the rights of students who are multilingual learners and/or immigrants. Research district policies, including any teacher handbook and/or evaluation system, that speak to the responsibility of serving and supporting multilingual learners across curriculum, instruction, and assessment. | |
| What are the state and federal laws that protect the rights of students who are multilingual learners, and/or immigrants? Do we know these laws well? Do our colleagues or leaders? Do we ever review these together? Why or why not? Whose responsibility is it to review? | | Identify dates on professional learning calendars that all staff are explicitly taught about federal and state laws that protect the rights of students who are multilingual learners and/or immigrants. Identify dates to annually review these laws, and incorporate this into any "new teacher" on-boarding. |
| Have I ever experienced linguistic oppression? Have my friends or family had this experience? | Listen. Listen to AND BELIEVE your students, families, colleagues when they share their lived experiences with you. Practice consent and respect their privacy without claiming their lived experiences as your own. | Conduct a Language Inventory in your classroom for your personal review. Identify a specific goal and a check-in date to monitor your own progress. |

*(Continued)*

**TABLE 2.3** (Continued)

| Question | Equip | Act |
|---|---|---|
| Have my current students experienced linguistic oppression in our community? How about in our school? Have our families? Have I ever witnessed linguistic oppression? What did I do or say? Why? Would I do anything differently now? What are the practices that I currently use or want to explore in order to actively incorporate the heritage languages of my students into our learning spaces? | Work with colleagues to identify resources and texts that provide representation of our students and others. Explore the ways your school promotes (or doesn't promote) multilingualism. | Ask members of the school staff or student body to conduct a Language Inventory of the School. Gather data, present the data, set a goal, and identify a check-in date to monitor the school's progress. |

# 3

# Affirming and Honoring the Linguistic Identities of Our Students

"Carly, your kids don't know my name!" the teacher down the hall expressed to me one October at lunch. "How do they not know my name? They just call me Teacher! It is just rude. They've made no effort to know my name and I've seen them once a week since the beginning of the year!"

I was surprised. "Really? They talk about you all the time—I've heard them mention you by name before!"

After hearing this, I decided I needed to review staff pictures with my students to ensure they knew the names of all of the folks they see most often. I put together a collection of photos that I pulled from our school website, and I outlined a few quick activities that we could do with those images.

When I first pulled up the pictures, my students all excitedly called out the names of every single adult, including this particular teacher. Confused, I just shrugged, and told my students that they rocked getting to know all of their teachers, and we moved on with the day.

A few weeks later, my students were with this teacher while I was in my classroom during a plan period. I saw that one of my students' parents dropped off their hoodie (which was a really important comfort item to them), so I decided to walk it down to this student during that class because I knew it would mean a lot to them.

When I walked in, they were all engrossed in a really cool learning experience, so I plopped down in a chair to enjoy it along with my students. All of a sudden, one of my students turns to my colleague and yells, "TEACHER! THIS IS THE COOLEST!" My colleague's eyes widened and she gestured to me, as if to say, "See? They don't know my name!"

Realization hit me like a brick, right in the head. Were you hit, too? If not, no worries. Let me explain.

The students I served in that class were all heritage Spanish-speakers, with families from places like Mexico, Guatemala, Venezuela, and Honduras (among others). It is customary for folks to use titles out of respect. For example, I would greet my doctor by calling them *Doctor* instead of Donna or Mrs. Johnson. In many Spanish-speaking countries, there is a lot of respect and esteem for teachers, so it's common to refer to teachers by their title—*Teacher*.

My colleague didn't know this. She interpreted their respect as disrespect. Woah!

After making this realization that day, I sat down with her and explained what was happening. She was absolutely mortified and felt really guilty about it. She said, "I've been teaching for over 20 years—how am I just learning this now?! I was assuming the worst, and they were literally honoring my role!"

Situations like these happen a lot. I know I've also experienced plenty of these moments. I've misstepped. I've made assumptions. I've gotten it wrong. Over and over and over again. For real! Again, I'm not a "bad teacher" or even a "bad person." But I did get stuff wrong, and I still get plenty of stuff wrong.

Can we chat about why?

When the diversity of our students and families doesn't match the demographics of the folks who work in the schools, a lot of work needs to be done. At an individual level, this requires us to get real and get honest about our own biases, our own beliefs and ideas, and our own understandings and misunderstandings of the world. When I start to bridge this conversation, I can recognize that this makes a lot of folks feel very uncomfortable.

Rather than shy away from that discomfort, I invite us to sit with it a little bit.

Sometimes, this internal unpacking is what provides us with the biggest insights to how we can address and assess our mindsets, actions, habits, and routines. I also want to acknowledge that this requires dedicated time and commitment to doing the work but also sitting with discomfort. Time is really hard to come by during the school year—and let's be honest, even during the summer months. During especially difficult seasons of the school year, we may be floating through seasons of pure survival. This makes doing the lifting of addressing bias feel "too much" for many. This is another reason why this work cannot simply be an initiative and instead must be baked into the fibers of our structures, routines, and habits throughout the year.

I can attest that understanding myself better has led me to approach others with a curiosity rather than a judgment. The more time I devote to understanding how my past, my personality, my positionality, my biases, my decisions, my mistakes, and even the mistakes of others have all influenced how I show up in different places and spaces, the more I am able to consider those pieces of other people and how *they* show up in different places and spaces.

## Cultural Competencies

As we serve and support multilingual learners across our communities, it's important to acknowledge that we may have limited understanding, and that's okay—as long as we remain committed to continual growth. Sometimes it's difficult to admit that we may be making a lot of assumptions about values.

The great thing about cultural competencies is that they are a collection of skillsets that all of us can work on and develop over time. Developing cultural competencies doesn't mean that you must be deeply educated beyond a superficial level about each unique culture of the world. It does mean that you are committed to learning and unlearning. It does mean that you can have wonderings, questions, and considerations. It also means that you can be wrong and then corrected over time!

When I work with schools and we talk about developing and nurturing our own individual and collective cultural competencies, there is often a misconception about what this might mean. To illustrate this point, I will turn to the Culture Tree by Zaretta Hammond. You might have heard of the Cultural Iceberg, which is often attributed to the work of E.T. Hall in 1976. The idea is that on the surface of the water—the visible parts of the iceberg on top of the water—lies what we all can easily see, hear, or experience across culture. These can include things like language, flags, dance, fine arts, food, and more. When we look beyond the surface and go underwater to identify the "deeper" layers of culture, we see things like expressions of joy, what constitutes demonstrations of respect, body language, views of mental health, concepts of wealth, eye contact, notions of beauty, and much more.

The "surface level" pieces are things that are highly praised during most schools' "International Night" experiences—where students or families each host a booth or a classroom, and share facts about their heritage country and culture. Now, I want to be clear here that these are all important pieces of culture! Just because it represents the "surface level" doesn't mean that these are wrong to celebrate or that they are unimportant. I also want to be explicit here that this is often where most schools stop conversations about culture. Celebrating surface-level culture can falsely provide educators, administrators, and leaders with the sense that they are building cultural competencies well enough to inform decision making, become more reflective practitioners, or move the needle of real change for equity and advocacy for multilingual learners (and all students).

The "deeper level" pieces are sometimes more difficult for folks to grasp, especially as we all have our own unique perspectives, upbringings, cultures, and opinions on each of those pieces. However, these pieces are incredibly important for us to explore, learn about, identify, and be curious about—these are the things that pop up most in expressed behavior concerns, discipline referrals, opinions discussed in a teacher's lounge, or conceptions of how "involved" families or caregivers are in their child's education. These are worthy of our time and attention! These are opportunities for us to address our biases, our misconceptions, our misunderstandings, our prejudices—and also to reckon with how each of these biases, misconceptions, misunderstandings, and prejudices have been cultivated, nurtured, and supported in our schools and systems (whether intentionally or unintentionally).

In her book *Culturally Responsive Teaching* and the Brain, Zaretta Hammond (2015) expresses a different representation of culture. Instead of an iceberg, she poses a Culture Tree. A tree is a living, growing being that grows, evolves, and changes over time. A tree exists with roots that may be intertwined with the roots of others. The "surface level" culture is represented in the leaves and blossoms on the tree, while the "deep level" culture is represented through the roots of the tree. She also takes the notion a step further by identifying the amount of emotional trust associated with each layer of culture.

When evaluation structures call on practitioners to be culturally responsive some folks misinterpret this with being culturally relevant, or providing learning experiences that are reflective of the diversity of their student population. When this happens, we see a lot of references to "heroes and holidays" or select texts that provide students with "exposure" throughout the course of a unit or school year. Mere exposure still centers one perspective. If we're still centering all of our learning experiences around a monolingual, white, cis gender, Christian, hetero mindset and framework, we are merely "adding on" an attempted layer of exposure. This is similar to the "After Slap" effect that we see in instruction for multilingual learners that we'll explore further in Chapter 4.

## Norms vs. Traditions/Holidays

Celebrating "heroes and holidays" seems to be an easier lift for educators and curriculum designers who fit the current norm and narrative in US education. *Did we host an International Night this year? Check! We're on our way! We're doing great! Now let's gear up for the same show next year!* Most educators I've worked with or supported over the years tend to highlight traditions and holidays rather than explore deeper levels of culture and learn about various cultural norms from around the world. Again, sometimes this may feel like an easier lift or feel "more fun" to learn about and bring into the classroom. However, deeper levels of culture and various cultural norms are important things to learn about and be better informed about because deeper levels of culture have greater impact on emotional trust between people, as illustrated by Zaretta Hammond's Culture Tree (2015).

Merely sticking to the "heroes and holidays" mentality impacts our perceptions of how inclusive we are as a school staff. If we just stick to surface levels of culture, then our inclusion efforts will remain only surface level. Deeper levels of culture show up in every facet of the schoolhouse, but we see the greatest impact at the decision-making tables, like when we meet to adopt a new SEL curriculum resource, host a data review meeting, a student problem-solving meeting, an eligibility meeting, and more.

Eye contact is one piece of "deeper culture" and I feel that this one seems to be a slightly more accessible entry point for a lot of teachers. For example, does eye contact signify that you're listening to the speaker for you, or does it denote a tone of disrespect or challenging authority? It can mean different things to different people! SEL programs are loaded with an over-hyped focus on making eye contact to "show respect" to the speaker (whether it's a peer or an adult), but this is highly problematic to have this as an "expected behavior" to kids where their culture or family might have different eye contact expectations.

Another example of SEL programs that suggest things that may be problematic includes "calm bodies" and "sitting still" on your chair or on the carpet. What if I can still listen and attend to learning while moving? This suggestion is quite ableist as well.

Consider your current staff. Do you have a lot of women on your staff? Then you may consider another potential entrance ramp for educators to begin these conversations. There was a clip I once saw on social media where someone went around and asked women what they'd do if there was a 7pm curfew for men. Some of the answers were rattling. They replied that they'd go for a run at night, they'd go to the gas station to fill up, they'd hit the grocery store, or that they'd take their kids out to dinner by themselves, if they knew there'd be no men outside. This means that these are all things that those women are fearful to do knowing that there are men in their community. I know this to be true for myself.

As a female, I recognize certain things that I do that are influenced by the existence of men. This is based on my own lived experiences, and also the things that I have been explicitly or implicitly taught. I only pump gas in my car during daylight hours. There are certain grocery stores that I will never visit again because of scary encounters that I've experienced there. When I'm parking my car in a large lot or parking garage, there are certain things that I am conditioned to do, like park under a light, locate the cameras, check my surroundings for ten seconds prior to leaving the car, and walk with my key between my fingers while I'm outside, etc. If I walk through a parking lot or parking garage and I see a man walking towards me, I look them in the eyes while making a note of their description (the color of their shirt and shorts, their hair color, their height), just in case. If you've ever been in a situation where you've had to provide authorities with the description of someone who caused you harm, you might do this, too.

Perhaps you've also seen the social media trend about women who walk or hike on trails. The question is posed if they'd feel safer with a bear on the path alone with them or a man. The answers were overwhelmingly leaning towards the bear. Isn't that something?

We give young women safety devices as holiday gifts, like mace and safety alarms. We even make them in pretty colors so they feel more fun to carry. When we teach our daughters how to drive, we teach them different tips and tricks than we teach our sons. When traveling recently with my daughter, she remarked to me as we left our hotel room, "We have to have more street smarts than guys."

Wow—was this something I told her out loud before? Was this something she was just noticing? Was this something she's seen on social media? Is this something she talks about with her friends?

## Our Names

Calling students by the names they prefer is important. Spending time at the beginning of the school year or semester is important, but that's where most teachers stop. Many teachers will tell students, "Please correct me if I say it wrong" in an effort to pronounce students' names correctly. However, our students may not be okay with correcting a teacher—it may conflict with their own cultural norms, or it may go against what they've been taught at home! Students are watching all our interactions carefully and how we respond to the "corrections" of students. Some students may not trust that it's safe to correct you, even if it's something they obviously know more about (like how to say their name!). It's wise to reserve a check-in a few weeks into the school year or semester to be sure we're getting it right. Keep it quick and keep it light. Don't go overboard apologizing if a student tells you seven weeks in that you've been mispronouncing their name this whole time. Apologize sincerely, practice it until it's right, then move on.

See Table 3.1 for a few quick picture books that highlight the importance of our names.

**TABLE 3.1** Books that Highlight the Importance of Our Names

| Book Title | Author |
|---|---|
| *Becoming Vanessa* | Vanessa Brantley-Newton |
| *Alma and How She Got Her Name* | Juana Martinez-Neal |
| *My Name Is an Address* | Ekuwah Mends Moses |
| *Say My Name* | Joanna Ho |
| *Your Name Is a Song* | Jamilah Thompkins-Bigelow |
| *Always Anjali* | Sheetal Sheth |
| *Yefferson, Actually/En realidad, es Yefferson* | Katherin Trejo and Scott Martin-Rowe |
| *The Boy Who Tried to Shrink His Name* | Sandhya Parappukkaran |
| *Teach Us Your Name* | Huda Essa |
| *That's Not My Name* | Anoosha Syed |

## The Underbelly of Relationships: Bias and Perception

Relationships between staff and students have been highlighted in countless research studies, social media posts, professional learning sessions, blogs, and professional books. Yes, relationships are absolutely important! From what I've consumed on this topic, the stress on relationships in our work has been focused mostly on adult behaviors while interacting and engaging with students. Our adult behaviors are within our control. Our adult actions can and do influence our relationships. However, I must also underscore how our mindsets, beliefs, and understandings also influence and impact our behaviors, and ultimately, our relationships.

The mindsets we hold absolutely shape our relationships. If I truly value the assets that each student brings into the learning space, I will adopt a healthy mindset about what the student is capable of—and the flipside also holds true. If I believe that the student possesses a "language barrier" or other "barrier," this will shape my mindset, my behaviors, my expectations, and my interactions with students.

Years ago, I interviewed multilingual middle school students about their perceptions of the adults in their classrooms, including their teachers, paraprofessionals, and school leaders. Students between 6th and 8th grades remarked on different perceptions through their interactions with various staff members in their school building. These were adults that they see every day. Some of their quotes will remain with me forever:

"He rolled his eyes at me when I spoke Spanish."

"She doesn't think I'm smart, so I just stay quiet in math."

"He knows science isn't my thing."

Again, these were their perceptions of the adults who were serving in the school. The first one especially struck me, especially as we explore our own linguistic identities, and those of our students. If this student observed this adult's behavior, what are they to believe? Is their heritage language (the language of their home and family) safe in the school? Is their identity fully embraced and welcomed in the school, or in the classroom?

The second quote also struck me as worrisome. Our students are always developing different parts of their identities, including who they are as readers, as scientists, as mathematicians, as computer scientists, etc. The fact that the student remarked (quite confidently) on their perceptions of their teachers' mindsets in a negative way is a huge cause for concern. Additionally, their perception of their teachers' mindset set forward an action on behalf of the student: *I just stay quiet in math*. For a group of students who have been historically underserved, silenced, and oppressed—this must call us all to action. We cannot afford to have our students feel silenced—especially by their teachers.

The third quote is also one that calls on us to do some uprooting: *He knows science isn't my thing*. The student that shared this waved it off as if it was common knowledge between him and his teacher. We need for every student to know that science, math, reading, writing, languaging, and education is their thing, too. I will be honest here and share that I've written myself off an embarrassing amount of times over the years, calling out that "I am not a creative person," or "I'm not a math person," or even, "I'm not a techy person." I have to be especially mindful as a female in education, with younger folks listening to me (even when I don't think they are). If I "bow out" of having math or science or technology as a part of who I am or what I'm capable of, it gives younger folks (and others) the permission to also do the same. All of us have the responsibility to be mindful of our language choices and how they impact those around us. Does this mean I'm passionate about math, science, or technology all of the time? Maybe not, but I can't let a young person hear me say that the entire field of math, science, or technology (or other field) is not for me. It's for all of us, and our students need to see themselves as having a space in every field. As they grow through their years in school and in life, they may develop their own unique passions and interests, which is great—but our mindsets influence our actions and interactions, which influence our relationships, which influence student perceptions.

If these young people are moving through their classes harboring these perceptions of what their teachers think about them, it influences how they show up in those content areas, and how they engage with those content areas. If their perceptions are negative, how does this influence their sense of belonging in that space?

Now yes, there's always more to the story. It's hard to identify what actions and interactions the students have had with their various teachers and leaders that would lead to the perceptions developing. For the first quote, was the teacher rolling their eyes at the student because they were speaking in Spanish? Or was the teacher rolling their eyes at something else at the exact moment that the student looked at them while also speaking in Spanish? I wasn't there, so of course I have no idea. However, it is important to note that most perceptions are not formed after just one interaction, but after many. Our brains are usually pretty good about collecting evidence through multiple interactions and experiences over time. No, this certainly isn't always the case (have you ever formed a mindset about someone based on a first impression?). This also makes me wonder about actions and interactions I've had over the years with students. What did they think that I believed about them? What evidence might they have to support those ideas? What was happening with my words, actions, and interactions? What did I explicitly say to them? What did I implicitly communicate to them? What might they have overheard me say when talking to another adult or another student? What nonverbals did they pick up on in my interactions (my posturing, my facial expressions, my gestures, my eye contact or eye behavior)? It makes me really understand just how important my words, actions, and interactions with each individual student are in my work across days, weeks, months, and years.

## Believing Students and Families' Lived Experiences

Earlier, as you read through those students' statements, were you immediately looking for ways to dismiss them? Or explain away why they may have said something? Why do you think that is?

This sounds very simple, but it's often overlooked. So let's say it. We have to BELIEVE students and families when they share their experiences, even when it's hard or painful to receive that information. We cannot immediately be defensive. If we are, we should spend some time sitting with that and asking ourselves why our immediate reaction is to be defensive.

As mentioned earlier, language has a big role in culture, and languaging has a large space of cultural competencies. Let's continue to explore our languaging stories, as one piece of our own cultural upbringing.

## Linguistic Journeys

Have you ever reflected on your own linguistic identity—or your linguistic journey? Have you ever acknowledged that you even have one? When I work with various schools and districts, we often can recognize that no one has ever asked us to reflect on this before. Unless we ourselves are multilingual, we rarely reflect on how we language across various contexts and situations. Folks who are monolingual have likely never been asked this question. Folks who are multilingual have likely had to do some type of reflection on their linguistic identity in their journeys—either as a response to facing linguistic oppression or trying to navigate life between two linguistic spaces.

Let me share a little of my own unique language journey. I grew up in a monolingual family on the north side of Chicago. If I were to walk down the block of my childhood, I'd hear neighbors utilizing languages like Italian, Polish, Spanish (Mexico), Spanish (Puerto Rico), Spanish (Guatemala), Russian, Bulgarian, Bosnian, and Tagalog—just to name a few. It was a linguistically rich neighborhood where languages lived in conversation, in the stores, in our radios, and on our TVs. Up through 8th grade, while we had lots of languages present in my classmates and families, all instruction at school was provided in English only—there were never links or connections to other languages (let alone world language class offerings, or even clubs).

My grandparents on my mother's side were from the South, and I adored their Southern accents. In fact, when I was little, I thought I'd eventually "grow into" my own Southern accent (this sadly never occurred). I learned that some of their language choices and expressions didn't always "translate" easily into conversations with folks in my school or neighborhood. For example, other kids didn't know what I meant when I said that I looked all over tarnation for my Lisa Frank Trapper Keeper but couldn't find it. They'd exchange glances and ask a clarifying question, "Does that mean your fronchroom?" I learned that languaging is influenced by regionalisms (front room + Chicagoese = fronchroom) and expressions (*all over tarnation*).

When we moved to the suburbs of Chicago for high school, I was able to start taking Spanish classes (as a world language—but back then, it was called a "foreign" language—which in itself is a great conversation about how we position languages). *It's important to call out that I learned an additional language out of a PRIVILEGE, not out of a necessity or need to navigate my school or community, or learn new content.* Most of my Spanish courses in high school were taught by folks who looked a lot like me but who participated in study abroad programs in their past. I would often have conversations at lunch and after school with my friends (many of whom were heritage Spanish languagers) and they would correct my Spanish so that it was more "real" and not "out of a workbook." I started to notice there were different functions and perceptions of language.

I continued my Spanish courses in college, but I never did a study abroad program—which sometimes led to uncomfortable conversations when it was assumed that anyone who'd major or minor in a language MUST HAVE done so at some point during their college years (no—this is very much not the case! That costs money!). My new college friends again supported my "real Spanish," which was a true privilege (thank you Zully, Karina, and Christina for helping me through Spanish literature courses!). When I started my student teaching program, I recognized the language privilege in classrooms in the city and suburbs and from private to public schools. I realized I could start to leverage my growing language skills in Spanish to support students who were new to the community.

When I first started my teaching career in the Chicago suburbs, I was happy to put my languaging skills to work to better serve and support students (and especially families)—and have those skills sharpened, refined, and in a constant state of growth. After my second year of teaching, those same (ever-growing, highly imperfect, still privileged) Spanish language skills became exploited. *I'd like to highlight here that later on in this chapter, I'll address how language skills of adult heritage speakers are exploited even further.*

I thought I should celebrate being moved from the mobile classroom in the parking lot to having a "real" (converted closet) classroom inside of the building—but it was explained that the rationale was that they needed to have someone who spoke Spanish near the front office. Interruptions to my teaching became a frequent occurrence—and while I was happy to serve families in our community, I felt that my service to students was impacted. I would receive phone calls or visits from the front office in the middle of lessons saying that they'd cover my class real fast while I went to interpret for a new family or hopped on a waiting phone call.

There were seasons throughout the school year where I would utilize more Spanish, like "parent-teacher" conference week (more on that name choice later on), or the months of August and May where we were registering families for the school year. During these seasons, I would start to dream in Spanish, which was super exciting to me. When I became a classroom teacher in a bilingual program, I used a lot of Spanish every day, which made my skills become much stronger. When I became a district-wide instructional coach, I used far less Spanish—and even today, my Spanish language skills are in constant fluctuations.

As an English languager today, I enjoy and prefer writing in informal, narrative tones via my blog posts, social media posts, text messages, and more. I overuse exclamation points constantly as well as emojis. I am a hardcore "expressive lengthener"—which I didn't realize was a real thing with a real name until I read the book *Because Internet: Understanding the New Rules of Language* by Gretchen McCulloch. If you're curious, this refers to the lengthening of certain letters to express big feelings, like *I'm sooooo excitedddd!!!* I have gone to great lengths to adjust this register for the sake of this book (you're welcome!!!!).

As someone who speaks a lot in my work, I have noticed that not everyone appreciates me pushing linguistic expectations just a little because I don't always speak in the tones or registers that some may expect from a "professional speaker." I frequently dance around, laugh at my own jokes, and lean a little informal.

It is important for every education practitioner to reflect on their languaging journeys. Doing so helps us to be better practitioners as we can start to recognize that every human being with whom we interact also has a very unique language journey. This means that our students (whether they are monolingual or multilingual) all have a unique story about their languaging. This means that each of our colleagues also has a unique language journey. Even if any two of us have a shared language, it doesn't mean that our language stories are the same.

As we explored earlier, linguistic oppression is a reality that many of us and our students have faced, and continue to face. A lot of us would be heartbroken to learn about the linguistic oppression of our students, the families we serve, our colleagues, our own friends and family members, and community members. While these moments in our journeys can be private (and it may be none of our business to ask individuals about), it is important that we recognize that these moments are real, and they are harmful. This makes it even more important that we unpack our own linguistic biases and build our own cultural competencies.

All of these elements of our journeys are things that we bring into our experiences at school and work. They can and do influence how we interact with others. They can and do influence our relationships with our colleagues as well as the students and families we serve. Our understanding of our linguistic identities can help us to recognize the linguistic identities of those we serve and those we serve alongside.

## Linguistic Familiarity, Linguistic Bonding, and Linguistic Bias

I feel an immediate sense of comfort and kinship to folks who have Southern accents, because my grandparents had Southern accents. Have you experienced a moment of linguistic bonding like this? I also feel an immediate sense of comfort and kinship to folks with very thick Chicago accents, because of my parents' thick Chicago accents. It feels familiar to me, like I'm "home." I don't even notice it or pay attention to it when I'm in the city or even in the suburbs and many folks around me have this accent, but if I'm on vacation somewhere or traveling for work to another state and I pick up on a Chicago accent from someone in the same space, I feel immediately bonded to that person even though we are complete strangers. This is an example of linguistic bonding.

This is similar to bonding over a shared love of something, like if my family was out and about and we noticed someone wearing an Ohio State Buckeyes t-shirt. Living in the Chicagoland area, this isn't something we see often, but it bonds us to that stranger when those moments happen. The linguistic bonding runs slightly deeper, because it ties us to deeper feelings of comfort, kinship, familiarity, and a sense of "home."

This is also an example of linguistic bias, because I may not experience that instant sense of kinship to someone with another accent. Does that mean I prefer to be with folks that sound like me? Or does it simply mean I notice it more? If my feelings are influenced or changed by my associations with different accents, this is an example of linguistic bias—meaning, *I have linguistic biases*. Wow!

Of course, this isn't to say that I never bond with folks with other accents. On the contrary! I have friends and family across tons of languages and accents, and we've bonded over lots of stuff—but I'm talking specifically here about that instant, implicit, automatic pull I feel when I hear a Southern accent.

Does this mean I'm a terrible person? No, probably not. It does mean I should be aware of this and acknowledge how it shows up in my life, especially in my work in serving students, families, and working alongside colleagues. It does mean I must continue my own self-work.

Linguistic bonding is actually really important. It's important for languages of all ages, but it's *especially important* for our young languagers. Our young people constantly play with language. As the mother of two teenagers, I learn new words and phrases from them all the time. At the time of this writing, "rizz" and "sigma" and "skibbidi" are all words frequently used and heard in my house (and in their schools and social groups). While these aren't words and phrases from my generation, I can remember the words and phrases that I used with my friends in my younger days (phrases like *"as if!"* or *"she's all that and a bag of chips!"*). Perhaps you've heard these words or phrases used by your students or other young folks in your life. Perhaps they give you a giggle or perhaps they drive you absolutely crazy.

What I want for us to remember is that students use these words and phrases *as a form of linguistic bonding*. This is important languaging that helps give them a sense of belonging to their peers. With this being said, let's address something specific. On social media, I've seen pictures that teachers have posted that have anchor charts with "banned word lists." These posters list all the different social languaging our young people use and enjoy using. Somewhere on the poster there's a message like "THESE ARE NOT ALLOWED IN ROOM 9!" And friends, this is an oppressive practice.

## Exploitation of Multilingualism

If you are multilingual, you may have had your linguistic skills exploited by your school or district. It never feels good. Earlier in this chapter, I shared how I felt that my language skills were being exploited. Again, I will note that privilege is an important piece to acknowledge here. Let's dissect the exploitation of languages a little further.

There are various roles within a school ecosystem. Some roles are designed solely for providing interpretation or translation. Most roles within a school system are not solely designed for this purpose, and all of these roles are enhanced when someone is multilingual. For example, when a classroom teacher within a monolingual program also speaks Russian, this is seen as a helpful resource to the teacher down the hall who has a Russian newcomer student and needs help with interpretation for parent-teacher conferences. When staff members who are multilingual are asked to translate or interpret and it falls outside of their initial job description, they must be compensated.

Treating their multilingualism as a "school or district perk" without properly compensating them for their time and skillset is exploitative. Assuming that they are going to lend the school or district their skills for free is exploitative. Asking multilingual staff members to "do it for the kids" or suggesting that "if they don't do it, no one else will" is both manipulative *and* exploitative.

## Voices from the Field

### *Anonymous EL Teacher*

> I was so excited to get my first real teacher job that I really tried to share all of my skills with the interviewing team. I told them that I spoke Spanish because I wanted it to give me an edge over other candidates. Spanish is a part of my family and I grew up bilingual. I knew that this school's community had a lot of Spanish-speaking students and families. I ended up getting the job, and after a few months, I hated it. I was constantly expected to "translate this real fast" even though it was never fast. Ten minutes here and there across a week adds up. I even stayed well beyond everyone else's parent-teacher conferencing hours because I had to translate for other families who I didn't even know. I was constantly asked by my principal and by my teammates to "just quickly" make this phone call or write this email.

> I was even asked to stand up next to my principal for our back-to-school night so I could interpret in front of everyone. I was so uncomfortable doing this because I don't like speaking in front of adults. The amount of extra work that all of this put on my plate was astronomical. I went to my teacher's union because it just became too much, but unfortunately they didn't really do much to help me and just told me I could decline the requests from my colleagues and my principal. I wasn't tenured, so I feared that if I told my principal (who was also my evaluator) that I didn't want to do this anymore, that I would get in trouble. I didn't want my teammates to be mad at me either. This in addition to other things made me feel like I wasn't being appreciated. I eventually left that school. When I was interviewing, I didn't volunteer this information to the team. On the digital application, I marked that I wasn't bilingual because I didn't want to get taken advantage of again. I felt like I had to protect my language and keep it a secret so that I could just focus on doing my job.

How do we treat our multilingual staff? How do we protect their multilingualism (and their linguistic identities) from being exploited? If you are in a leadership role, it is your responsibility to have structures set up for interpretation and translation for your school community. More information on the civil rights of families to have language access can be found in Chapter 7. Perhaps you have a dedicated interpreter or translator role for the school or district. Perhaps you have a multifaceted role that comes in the form of a multilingual family liaison. Or perhaps you invest in contracting with language services. In addition, you must also clearly communicate this structure and process so that neither you nor your multilingual staff is exploited in this way. Identify compensation structures and secure funding for this so that this structure is protected.

If you are the colleague or teammate of a multilingual staff member, don't assume that the multilingual staff member is always available or willing to interpret or translate. Go to your leadership, union, or human resources department to ask how to go about securing language access for your students or families. To be an ally to your multilingual colleague or teammate, shut down requests when you see or hear it happen. "Frank, don't ask her to translate for you. You have to contact the district translator. Do you want me to send you their email address?"

## Voices from the Field

### *Anonymous Dual Language Teacher*

> I once worked at a school district where I was the only Latina. A lot of the school's student population was also Latino, so I was surprised when I realized that there were literally no other staff members in our district that were like me. We had a small dual language program but all the other dual language teachers were white and Spanish was their second language. I really liked the community and I loved my kids and their parents. Most of my teammates were nice, but every now and then I'd hear something said about our Latino/a students that kind of rubbed me the wrong way.
>
> I started to notice that the person who runs our school social media account would make an effort to feature me in the school's online posts. At first it felt nice but after a while it really felt like they were putting me up so much not because of the work that I was doing but because it was trying to showcase how "diverse" our staff was—and it really wasn't diverse. We once had a conversation about attracting more diverse people for hiring in the future, and that kind of cemented my thinking about them.

> I left after two years. It wasn't just that situation, but there was just always this feeling I had that I was supposed to "represent" for the whole Spanish-speaking community all by myself.

Are we "othering" our colleagues, teammates, and leaders because of their linguistic identity? Are we expecting them (either explicitly or implicitly) to represent an entire community? No one should ever be expected to independently serve an entire community because of their identity.

It is especially important to be aware of our treatment of teammates and colleagues when we have bilingual and dual language programs that are partnered with monolingual classrooms. For example, I was a third grade dual language teacher for six years. I was on the 3rd grade team that consisted of anywhere between five and eight monolingual 3rd grade classrooms depending on the year, and my class was the only dual language class.

Because the team that I worked with was very supportive, they would ask questions at staff meetings about language access on my behalf—so that I wouldn't have to. This was always one small move that had a huge impact for me individually. I'll also point out that this eventually became the culture and climate of the building, where our leadership wouldn't even share information about upcoming outgoing communication until it was available in multiple languages, so that when it was presented, they'd share, "This is our multilingual communication for families about. . ."

I can recognize that my personal and social identity matter here. My colleagues and I all had similar social identities on that team. I often wonder if my social identity was different, how would I perceive them asking about language access on my behalf? For me, I was thankful, and I told them that.

However, in other contexts with other factors of social identity at play, I absolutely hate feeling that someone is speaking for me or those I serve. I find it insulting and disrespectful. For example, if a man reports out at a book study what it's like to be a female in a male-dominant field based on his perspective, I might question his intent. How could he possibly speak to a female's lived experience?! My reaction probably depends on what exactly he was saying or sharing. Statements like "Women in this field should . . ." might be perceived differently than "I'm going to listen and learn from the women in this space. I can . . ." Context certainly matters!

The linguistic identities of staff can also intersect with the various roles and positions within a school system. Let's read about one assistant principal's noticings about a specific role in their school.

## Voices from the Field

### *Anonymous Assistant Principal*

When I first started working as an assistant principal for an elementary school, I was committed to learning every staff member's name. Of course, you've got to learn the first and last names of everyone, since our "teacher names" are what our students use! In my first few weeks, I noticed that everyone referred to each other by Mr., Mrs., Ms., or Doctor Last Name—everyone except for our custodian. Our custodian was referred to by Mr. First Name. I thought this was strange. I'll also note that he was the only staff member of color at this school. He shared the same language as many of our students. All the kids and teachers absolutely loved him. One day I asked him, "Why don't the kids call you Mr. Last Name?" and he just laughed and said, "It's okay! I've always been Mr. First Name!" and we moved on. I went to the principal and asked her about it, and she admitted she never even thought about it. The next week, I walked past his office and saw that the sign outside of his office was changed to Mr. Last Name.

> Throughout the year, my principal would highlight different staff members on social media and in our family newsletters. I noticed that when she highlighted him later in the year, she referred to him as Mr. Last Name.
>
> I'll always wonder why that had been the norm and if anyone ever pointed that out before.

## Addressing Inclusion and Our Own Leanings

Most educators and leaders that I've worked with over the years have expressed their interests and desires in having more inclusivity in classrooms and schools. However, at the time of this writing, some schools and districts (and yes, entire states) have pushed back on any efforts towards developing and nurturing inclusive spaces in schools. When we talk about Inclusion, what do we mean?

Because I have spent my career serving multilingual learners, my mind and heart naturally lean into the idea of *linguistic inclusivity*. Other colleagues with other areas of expertise naturally lean into inclusion for neurodiverse students, or students with diverse learning needs. Others might lean into inclusion for other student groups. These leanings can also absolutely come from our own personal and social identities. Where might you lean? What might you lean towards most when you hear the word *inclusion*?

Inclusion at its heart is ALL of this and much more, right? We want to nurture and cultivate inclusivity for ALL students and families that we serve. If this is not even a basic desire (let alone an actual focus) for any one of us, we're missing the mark. It is important for us to acknowledge our initial leanings. For me, I can acknowledge that I naturally tend to focus more on linguistic inclusivity. This means that I need to be cognizant of what I need to lean more into so that I can be a more inclusive educator for all I serve. If my natural inclination is to focus on linguistic inclusivity, I must continue to grow my awareness, understanding, learning focus, and advocacy efforts into inclusivity for other named student groups. Does this mean that I'm a bad person? Again, no. But it *does* mean I need to continue my growth and my learning trajectory.

To be inclusive, what does this mean? I think if we all sat down, we could unpack that word differently. We can talk about the internal work on our mindsets and beliefs. We could discuss the external work of our words, actions, interactions, and the goals we have for each of those either individually or collectively as teams or schools.

## Linguistic Identities and Linguistic Inclusivity

Through the lens of linguistic inclusivity, what might this mean? First, it may mean doing more reflective work about our own individual language journey and language identity. It may also mean learning about the unique language journeys and language identities of students and families we serve. It may mean building up our own understanding of language across various languages (things like vocabulary, discourse, syntax, grammatical transfers, cultural and societal norms of social and academic language, etc.).

In our classrooms, linguistic inclusivity may mean creating dedicated time and space (both physical space and also airspace) to honor our language identities in our content learning and our expressions of learning. For example, if you have a physical (or digital) space in your classroom for a word wall or anchor charts, are these only presented in English? Or do you have a multilingual word wall?

During moments where students have to record themselves speaking or reflecting, is there an opportunity for students to do that in the language of their choice? When students are partnering or working in small groups and they have a shared language other than English, are they invited and encouraged to use the language of their choice? *Woah, woah, Carly. Slow down. I don't share that language. How will I know if they're on task?* Don't worry reader, I'll get to this, too!

Linguistic inclusivity means that I do the work and I don't see it as going the extra mile. If I don't share a language with those I serve, but I want to be able to utilize something like a multilingual word wall, you have some options! This might be a moment where you tap into the linguistic powers of those around you, including students, families, colleagues, neighbors, or a professional interpretation or translation service.

Linguistic inclusivity also means that we have to continuously uproot our own feelings of discomfort. Does hearing your students conversing in a shared language that you don't have make you uncomfortable? Why? Perhaps it's that you're worried they're talking about something else, like what they did over the weekend, or something they saw online recently. Can I let you in on a little secret? Kids do this all the time anyway. So do adults. This is a very natural and social thing for humans to do. So take a deep breath! What are the things that you likely already do to help all kids stay on task for a particular task or a specific block of time? Perhaps you give students a few minutes to check in with each other as they enter the room. Maybe you set a timer for a few minutes to engage socially while they're settling in for the morning or the afternoon, so that they have protected time to be human beings before expecting them to be mathematicians. After providing instructions to students with the expectation that they'll get right to work, you might notice a group or two that is struggling with task initiation. Maybe you'll walk over and use that proximity as a prompt for them. Maybe you'll share a probing statement or question, like, "What will you do first as you are getting started?" or "Who will grab the materials we need?" to get them going in the right direction.

Perhaps though, your discomfort stems from the idea that maybe the students are talking about you, or another student in class. Uh-oh, here comes another secret. Kids do this all the time anyway, even in a shared language. Shocking, right? Humans are just wild! Even so, if I continue to cultivate learning spaces built on mutual respect and linguistic inclusivity, I'd be hopeful that our collective behaviors (our actions and interactions) can serve as a model for each other.

I personally would rather tell my students (both explicitly and implicitly) that I trust them and value their language enough to actively and repeatedly invite it, encourage it, and welcome it into our shared space, even if it's a language I don't share. I would rather a pair of students speak in their shared language about me once or twice (or even dozens of times) than telling a pair of students ever that their language is not welcome in our classroom. How about you? Perhaps they did need to express a shared moment about me, and they were trying not to hurt my feelings: maybe my hair was messed up, or perhaps they may exchange a quick, *OMG I think there might be something in Mrs. Spina's teeth!* (yes, that happens sometimes!) or maybe they're having a shared reaction about something that was said in class. Sure, go for it students!

Now, I know I'll get this question so let's talk about it. What if we believe that students are using a shared language as a veil to talk about other students (without that shared language) in class? Great question, because as we advocate for linguistic inclusivity, we don't want others to feel excluded. Setting and identifying collaboratively constructed norms alongside students can aid in this process. Collaboratively checking in and revisiting co-constructed norms with all students several times throughout the semester is a healthy practice for checking in on processes and flow, but also for the culture and climate of our classrooms. Let's also ensure that we're not making assumptions about what students might be talking about.

The key to linguistic inclusivity is both reflecting on our beliefs and mindsets and then also taking action. What is the evidence that I am being linguistically inclusive? I can put other languages on the walls but if I roll my eyes when students are speaking either socially or about content in their shared language, am I actually being linguistically inclusive? No, I'm not. We can't rely on just being a reflective practitioner alone. There must be actions that are a result of our reflections. Let's talk about a few potential actions or indicators that you are being linguistically inclusive.

- ◆ The learning space has physical representation of languages other than English. You often say out loud, "Please do this in the language of your choice." Your learning space is audibly multilingual.
- ◆ You monitor your non-verbals when students are speaking languages that you don't share. You are in tune with your own body language and facial expressions.

- When you can and when it's appropriate, you utilize translation for instructional purposes. You utilize tech tools to increase linguistic access in your learning space.
- You encourage colleagues and teammates to utilize multilingual presence (audible and physical) in their classrooms and in common areas.

Carly, why didn't you mention providing language access to family members, guardians, or caregivers when you listed a few ways to be linguistically inclusive? Did you forget to mention that? Thanks, friend. I didn't forget. I left it off the list entirely, because this is a basic right to all families in our schools. To not provide interpreters is a violation of a family or guardian's civil rights. To be in bare-bones-basic compliance with the law, in my opinion, isn't a shining pillar and example of being linguistically inclusive. It's just literally following the law. We'll talk more about this in Chapter 7!

## Perceptions of Language Programming

Some families will refuse, decline, or reject language support services through a multilingual program. As we unpack language identities, and the lived experiences of those around us (like the families we serve), we might consider the reasons why some families may refuse services.

First—yes, it's important to note that students, families, and staff members may all have different understandings of the programming available to multilingual learners. Schools should be very clear and transparent with all stakeholders about each program's goals and methods.

While we want to communicate that our linguistic identities are an important piece of who we are, and that multilingualism is an amazing gift, we also have to reckon with the fact that many families have experienced linguistic oppression in their lifetimes as well. They may have had experiences as a child that they don't want their own child to experience. Perhaps they were a part of a program that was completely separate from what their peers were doing and this made them feel "othered" by the school (staff, students, community, and even access to opportunities).

If your school has a high number of "parent refusals," this is important to explore. Having a strong relationship with our communities can allow us to have already-existing channels of communication. Understanding their why is important, but honoring their privacy and experiences is also important. We can't act like we know better.

Declining services as a parent/guardian/caregiver might be an act of advocacy on their part: *I am ensuring my child doesn't face the same discriminatory exclusion that I faced when I was a student in a program with the same name.* Sometimes, a family member may have been misinformed about multilingualism by a pediatrician or speech pathologist. Maybe they were told that speaking an additional language would confuse their child. These are great opportunities for real conversations.

## Voices from the Field

### *Karina Paul, EL Coordinator*

J is one of my favorite students to talk about. He had beginning English skills so he was placed in my bilingual 1st grade classroom. His mom spoke to me at the beginning of the school year about his struggles in reading and writing (he couldn't yet!). During the Covid pandemic her son lost so much foundational instruction. I reassured her that many students all across the world were probably in the same boat as J. She was even more worried about the fact that he was being taught in a bilingual classroom. She asked me if I thought it was a good idea to pull him out and put him in an all English classroom so he wouldn't be so behind. Again, I reassured her that J would be fine in my

> classroom. His first language was Spanish, and if we build on his native language, research says that his reading skills would transfer over to English. I also told her that Spanish is so phonetic, that it is much easier to learn than English. J would be getting English Language Development (ELD), so he would also receive English instruction. I also asked her to read with him in Spanish every night for 20 minutes. She took my advice and kept him in my classroom and supported him at home. By the end of the year, J was reading above grade level in Spanish, he would write amazing stories during Writers Workshop and he was transferring his reading skills in English. J's mom couldn't believe how great he did in our first grade classroom. She was impressed that he was starting to develop his English reading skills so quickly. Sometimes our bilingual parents need assurance that when given the right tools and providing support at home, their children can truly become bilingual.

## Exploring the Multilingual Learner Identities and Experiences Through Picture Books

There is a large collection of picture books that can help us to illustrate our students' and families' current and past linguistic identities and experiences. Others share the journey and perspective of newcomer students. Some explore the phenomenon of generational language loss (where grandparents, parents, or other caregivers don't share the same language as their grandchildren or children). These may be books that we utilize as we engage with this work at various stages—whether we are trying

**TABLE 3.2** Books That Feature Various Multilingual Identities and Experiences

| Book Title | Author |
| --- | --- |
| Drawn Together | Minh Lê |
| Marisol McDonald Doesn't Match/ Marisol McDonald no combina | Monica Brown |
| The Notebook Keeper: A Story of Kindness from the Border | Stephen Briseño and Magdalena Mora |
| Mango Moon: When Deportation Divides a Family | Diane de Anda |
| Wishes | Mượn Thi Văn |
| Where Butterflies Fill the Sky: A Story of Immigration, Family, and Finding Home | Zahra Marwan |
| My Two Border Towns | David Bowles |
| Con Mucho Amor | Jenny Torres Sanchez |
| Between Us and Abuela: A Family Story from the Border | Mitali Perkins |
| Nami's New Friend | Mandy Namjou Yom |
| Amy Wu and the Warm Welcome | Kat Zhang |
| Everything is Different Here. Again. Welcoming Gustavo/Todo es diferente aquí. De nuevo. Le damos la bienvenida a Gustavo. | Valerie Butron and Dr. Rita Guzman |

to engage a colleague in initial conversations or make wide-scale changes within our systems. See Table 3.2.

## Let's Go!

Exploring the multiple layers of our personal, social, and linguistic identities is important. Our biases are important to be aware of and actively confront. Our biases don't necessarily mean that we are bad human beings, but it means that we all have some uprooting to do! Our biases influence our interactions with those around us. Our interactions impact our relationships with our colleagues, our students, and our families. We can all Question, Equip, and Act on our biases, interactions, and relationships on our teams, in our schools, and within the greater school community.

Let's go! Let's Ignite Real Change!

**TABLE 3.3** Question, Equip, Act (Chapter 3)

| Question | Equip | Act |
|---|---|---|
| Is it hard or uncomfortable for me to talk about bias? Why or why not? | Gather more information about the languaging preferences of your students, families, and colleagues. | Explore your school or district's professional learning calendar. Review when/where you can dedicate time and space for work on developing and strengthening cultural competencies. |
| Have I ever interviewed current or former students about their experiences at school? What might they say? What have they said? Did I believe them? Did it change or inform any actions? Why or why not? | Start noticing when you have certain linguistic preferences or leanings. Unpack why that might be. Unpack how that might impact your work with those you serve. | |
| Am I comfortable when other folks around me engage with each other in a language I don't share? Why is that? Am I comfortable when students engage with each other in a language I don't share? Am I fearful they're talking about me? Why or why not? | Language with those who language differently than you. Listen to podcasts, watch movies or television shows, engage in conversations, etc. | Identify your own list of tools and resources that prioritize and center the multilingual perspective. Ban the "banned word lists." Create opportunities for students to language across genres, registers, and languages. Lean into your linguistic creativity with students: "What's another way we can express this idea?" |
| Have you experienced linguistic bonding? Have you explored the linguistic bonding of your students? What words or phrases bond them? | | |
| Have you ever reflected on your own linguistic journey as a languager? Who or what shaped who you are and how you language today? | | |

# 4

# Ensuring Equity and Access for Multilingual Learners at Tier 1

A strong tier 1 for multilingual learners is every adult's responsibility. Full stop. The art teacher. The biology teacher. The consumer sciences teacher. The ELA teacher. The teacher with the EL endorsement. The teacher without the EL endorsement. The principal. The instructional coach. I meant what I said: EVERYONE. Sometimes folks want to skip over this part. We absolutely cannot.

## Variances in Programming

We have varying program models in our schools, one of which is a Transitional Program of Instruction, or TPI. This feels like what maybe a lot of us grew up with when we were students or perhaps this is the model that our school uses today. Its goal is English proficiency. This is what most programs in the US have historically used as an "English as a Second Language" (ESL) class. These programs can offer a variety of either in-class support, out-of-class support, collaborative teaching, or co-teaching.

Another program model is Bilingual Education, which can be delivered through a variety of ways. Some Bilingual programs offer "early exit" or "late exit" which refers to the grade level where students make larger shifts toward all-English instruction. Bilingual programs often have language allocation plans where part of their day, or specific classes, are delivered in English and others are delivered in the additional language. Within this model, the goal is still English proficiency, but targeted efforts are made to transition students towards that by leveraging their heritage language first.

Dual Language Programs are also an offering in some schools. *One-way* and *two-way* refer to the student makeup of those classes. A one-way model means that the entire student population of that class are heritage speakers of another language, and English is their additional language. A two-way model means that the class is made up of 50% heritage English speakers and 50% additional language speakers. Both models have a goal of biliteracy.

Across each of these programs, teachers can provide language support through a variety of service delivery models including out-of-class support, in-class support, collaborative teaching, or co-teaching.

## Curricular Resources

With all the differences and variations in program models and service delivery models, it's important to identify who makes decisions about tier 1—namely, curricular resources. I'm so over the "representative groups" who pilot a program and collect data about how an already privileged student group performs using it and then how the program fakes like it was designed for "all learners," with catchy buzzwords and phrases enough so that the privileged white men in suits can make a decision about how many tens of thousands to devote to the for-profit curriculum company. Does that annoy you, too? Also, if you are a privileged white man in a suit who makes these decisions, I hope you're leveraging the expertise and opinions of those smarter than you.

Even more fun is when the program boasts little ugly gray boxes in their teachers' manuals about how this lesson can be "tweaked" to "adjust" for certain groups of learners. Has anyone ever told them that multilingual learners are anything but a homogenous group? Has anyone sat them down to have a heart to heart about how tweaks perpetuate systems of oppression for an already marginalized group? When I see those ugly boxes that suggest "tweaks," I see a gigantic red flag. You should, too. Here's why: By acknowledging that this lesson needs tweaking for an entire student group, they're already admitting that 100% of their lessons were not designed with our students in mind AT ALL—rather, they were a complete and utter afterthought. I'm over it. I call bullshit.

Not only that, but the tweaks they most often suggest are honestly a joke. Most of the time, publishers will just say something overly simplistic like, "Add a word bank," or "add a visual." I don't think those two suggestions that can fit inside a 2 inch by 2 inch text box are going to do much to really make a strong impact on our students. Instead of being embarrassed by these gray boxes, they're weirdly proud of them. Mmkay. Great job boasting about how ignorant you are in meeting the needs of all students.

Tweaks and band-aids have never served anyone. In fact, I think they undermine equity work entirely. They position true accessibility as something you can just fix with a word bank or a visual, and decision-makers buy it (both literally and figuratively). I think it's garbage that the companies offer fake solutions like this. I think more people need to call it out. We need to demand better of those folks and those companies. They have all the money in the world to hire experts to design meaningful curricular resources and tools to support all students, and the best they can come up with is to suggest a word bank or visual. Maybe they should Google some basics. Maybe they should use AI to investigate a little further. Or maybe they can just be real with folks and put honest phrases on their promotional materials that say, "This is probably going to be just fine for your privileged student groups in schools." At least then they'd have more integrity.

And this is just brushing the surface here for students who are in English language acquisition programs. Let's also acknowledge the curricular programs that claim to teach biliteracy. Oof. Buckle up friends, because now I'm agitated.

## Curricular Resources for Biliteracy

There are companies out there selling materials for "biliteracy" with no one who even works there full time who has taught for biliteracy, or even studied it, or maybe they've never even Googled it. Their understanding of biliteracy is that you teach English language skills and you translate some convenient parts in Spanish. Oh yes, you noticed it too, didn't you? *They haven't even thought of supporting other languages, even though our country has loads of other languages in bilingual and dual language programs, aside from Spanish.* Once the curriculum director (who didn't think to include the language director in this decision, if there even is such a position in the district) signs on the dotted line and orders all the materials, and teachers start to unbox all of it and unpack the components, they're forced to ask their evaluators, "Is this what we're supposed to use to teach literacy?" to which the directors excitedly say, "YES! We told them that we have a bilingual program and THIS RESOURCE COMES IN SPANISH! Yay for us!" What the curriculum developers and the district-level decision-makers failed to realize is that biliteracy programs require us to consider how to develop two unique sets of literacies, and not merely translate *some* of the stuff in a superficial way.

## Other Translated Curricular Resources

Should we go there now? Sure, why not. The translations that were "developed" by word-to-word technology-generated tools are such a slap in the face. Truly. With all of the multilingual human beings in the world, you mean to tell me they couldn't find a trained professional multilingual translator? No. I don't believe that's actually the case. It's that they didn't want to invest the time or effort. For real! And honestly, why would they?! They have been getting away with this as a practice for decades! Why change now? All they have to do is slap a sticker on their marketing boxes and that's all they need to do to pull the wool over the eyes of the decision-makers (aka Check Signers) who shouldn't be these decision-makers.

Also, did we check to see if everything (like, all the components of the program—from the lessons to the homework to the family/guardian unit letters, etc.) was even translated, or did they just translate what they claimed or deemed to be "essential?" Because let me tell you, that was a fun experience for the third grade bilingual classroom teacher who found out that "the Spanish materials are coming in 1–3 years but their district was one of the early adopters of this new updated set of resources! Isn't that exciting?!" This meant the third grade bilingual classroom teacher had to spend hours and hours (and HOURS) of unpaid extra overtime TRANSLATING each lesson and homework page, only to have the company "proudly release" the Spanish version of their math resources 3.5 years later, when they actually already did all of that work for free, so that their students wouldn't have inequitable experience at the hands of the curriculum company nor directors who made the purchase.

### Reasonable Demands for Translated Curricular Resources

Sidenote, if the program claims to be "available in other languages," you are owed about 37 really specific follow-up questions.

> **Demand quality of content.** Ask specifically about biliteracy skills. If your district offers an English/Spanish biliteracy program, ask them to show you how they incorporated English Language Standards and skills, Spanish Language Arts Standards and skills, and metalinguistic connections (aside from just random lists of cognates in their glossaries, because a list of cognates isn't the same as metalinguistic learning opportunities. They're a definite starting point, but this still tasks the teacher with doing the work, while monolingual teachers don't have that extra work).
> 
> **Demand quality of language.** Ask specifically about how the translations were developed.

**Demand equity.** Ask about which components of the program are translated by a human, and also ask which pieces are not translated by a human. If this is a program that is promising "authentic" materials, ask what language the text was originally written in.
**Demand the same timelines.** If the company comes out with the English version and they have a different timeline for their other languages, don't purchase the shiny new stuff until it's ready for everyone in your district. Reject putting that on your teachers. They're teachers—not translators.

If they don't offer these things at a bare minimum, walk away. What else might you add to this list of demands?

## Using a Curricular Resource "With Fidelity"

Fidelity is one of my least favorite words in education, because it's often accompanied by a scripted curriculum with rigid methodologies and 183-step lesson plans, all meant to serve hypothetical children who are NOT multilingual learners. If the program wasn't designed with fidelity, meaning it was only normed for a privileged group of learners to begin with (which doesn't match the actual real human children in our real-life classrooms), then screw fidelity.

If you, the curriculum resource company, or you, the director/evaluator, tell me that I am not ALLOWED to be responsive to the needs of my students based on the data I am receiving, then I don't really believe that YOU are doing YOUR JOB with fidelity.

## The After Slap

I could go deeper here, but for the sake of painting a full picture, let's move on. Let's say the district decision-makers purchase a resource chock-full of the cute little "tweaks" they love so much.

The gray box mentality has unfortunately trickled down into unit design and lesson design, even when teachers are tasked with individually or collaboratively creating their own materials. The "tweaks" come forward here, too. The problem with the gray boxes, the tweaks, and the band-aids is that we're not planning with language at the forefront. I call this The After Slap. First, we design the stuff—the content, the learning activities, the lessons. Then, we simply "slap on" a few tweaks and sprinkle those throughout the lessons and unit. We save the language needs as an afterthought. We don't do this because we're bad people. We're not bad educators. We are existing (and perhaps, just trying to survive) within a system that was designed to leave certain students out, and we aren't equipped with the time, the professional learning, the support, or the non-negotiable expectation that we plan with language at the forefront instead of leaving it as an afterthought as we've done for . . . well, forever.

Our schools must do better than The After Slap. We must demand that we do better.

## Civil Rights of Dually Identified Students

No, IEP needs don't "trump" language learning needs. They're both needs. They're both required by law to meet. I've had countless conversations with folks who misunderstand that an IEP is prioritized over linguistic needs because it's a legal individual plan signed off by a team, including family/guardians, and if it's not met, it's litigious. Someone could sue the district. But friends, violating the civil rights of a student is also litigious. Yep, it sure is. Meaning that if we're not providing for the full linguistic needs of our students, we are in violation of our students' civil rights. That is against the law. Not only that, but doing something (that we should be doing) just to avoid a lawsuit isn't really where our focus should be. We should be doing the right things because those are THE RIGHT THINGS to do. We must fully understand the civil rights of all students, especially when it comes to linguistic needs and providing linguistic access. We shouldn't have the permission to "opt out" because we don't have the English Learner / English as a Second Language endorsement or certificate. It is everyone's responsibility to know and understand our students' civil rights. Finally, prioritizing one set of student needs at school (like only prioritizing the IEP needs in scheduling/instruction/assessment), just because we're unfamiliar with civil rights law is not only inequitable and problematic, it's educational malpractice.

One issue I see most educators struggle with when students are dually identified is the scheduling. When I say dually identified, they have both linguistic needs (identified by the state as being a multilingual learner) and an IEP, or perhaps they have linguistic needs and are also eligible for acceleration/enrichment (or a combination of all three). Scheduling can be a challenge but it can also be an opportunity to collaborate. When teams are working together to determine a class placement, we do need to look at how we deliver services to students with multiple needs.

## Language Data and Shared Responsibility of All Staff

It is important that every teacher sees themselves as a language teacher. After all, everyone is teaching their content through languaging of some sort—often a combination of reading, writing, listening, and speaking. Every student we serve is also languaging as they process their learning and express their learning—again, this is often a combination of reading, writing, listening, and speaking. This means that yes, all educators are language teachers, and all students are language learners. Even our monolingual students are growing in their languaging skills throughout their days and years inside and outside of school.

Language support cannot be solely the responsibility of the EL teacher. Instead, every adult who serves at the school must be committed to serving the linguistic needs of their students. We can continue to foster this sense of shared responsibility by looking at our evaluation processes, our professional learning opportunities, and the way in which we speak about language data.

Language data does not represent the performance of an EL teacher. Rather, language data is schoolwide data. Consider for a moment that if your school has 1–2 EL teachers with a caseload of 67 students (likely more) across multiple grade levels, these 1–2 teachers likely have an overpacked schedule bouncing from classroom to classroom or from resource block to resource block. These 1–2 teachers cannot follow all their students to all their classes to ensure that their students' linguistic needs are being met in every content area. So, when we receive and review language data, this must be a shared experience that all staff understand is a reflection on how the entire school experience is serving and supporting their linguistic needs.

Language data in all forms (an annual assessment, a trimester- or semester-based EL progress report, or specific language captured through a speaking recording or written sample in PE or science) represents how the entire school staff serves the linguistic needs of all students. This means that the entire staff must have frequent opportunities to reflect on linguistic performance and linguistic goal setting. From the art teacher, to the fine arts department, to the science department, to consumer sciences—every adult plays a role in their student's language development.

## Professional Learning

Does your school make you attend mandatory training on how to use the laminator, but it doesn't offer a mandated (or even optional) training on the civil rights of our students and families? Think about it—when was the last time your staff learned about Plyler vs. Doe? When's the last time you reviewed language access for families? Seriously. Write down the date on a Post-It. I'll wait.

Ongoing professional learning for supporting multilingual learners should be required. This again shouldn't be something that folks can "opt in" or "opt out" of, as every adult must be held accountable for serving and supporting all students.

Remember, this doesn't just mean a workshop. Professional learning comes in many formats, shapes, and sizes. Sometimes it's a book study! Sometimes it's an article study. If you don't have time for that, do a quote study or a graphic study. Go for a walk outside or inside the school building and have folks listen to a podcast. Create a structure for peer-to-peer observations. Try to do site visits to other schools inside or outside of your district. Network by connecting with your regional office of education, emailing your nearby districts and striking up a conversation, or joining different social media groups. It's important to have varied methods for engaging in professional learning.

Strategy sessions feel good because they feel obtainable. They feel like something we can learn, practice, and apply. It's especially a great feeling when we can see that the strategy is doing what we intended for it to do—namely, provide language access to the multilingual students that we serve. I do tons of these types of workshops, because I think there is something to be said for educators feeling equipped—and I do think this can be one (yes, just one) way to feel equipped. However, we can't stop here.

One reason I believe that we tend to stop here is time. We don't have the time needed to do the background work of analyzing WHY our current structures (including unit design, lesson layout, curricular resources, pacing guides, etc.) are not *already* serving multilingual students. This is an important step to acknowledge the full scope of work that must be done.

Another reason we tend to stop at strategies is expertise. The folks who are leading, planning, or budgeting for professional learning often don't have the expertise in serving and supporting multilingual learners and/or equity for multilingual learners. Sometimes these folks will ask their EL staff to run professional learning sessions. While I believe that EL teachers are instructional leaders, I also want to acknowledge that this can be problematic. For one, not all teachers want to do this, especially when they're already stressed enough with their workloads and are not receiving any extra compensation for this. Second, not all EL staff feel equipped or comfortable in doing this, or they just don't want to—and that's valid. Third, not all EL staff should—not only because it's not their job, but sometimes it's a case of inherited problematic practices or outdated and/or debunked methodology. The EL teacher may not actually be EL-conscious. GASP! I know. But as I mentioned earlier, it happens.

If we fail to move beyond just professional learning on strategies alone, we are continuing to put band-aids on the deeper level of analyzing and disrupting the barriers that are perpetuated in our schools and systems. We must not only have conversations about the barriers we've either inherited, created, or contributed to perpetuating, but we must get serious about addressing the "what now—now that we are aware, what is our plan to restructure?" We are just as guilty as the textbook companies and instead are using the band-aid of "strategies" or those dreaded gray boxes in the teachers' manuals.

## EL and Bilingual Endorsements

There has been a huge demand across the US for more EL-certified teachers. States have begun fast-tracking endorsement course programs to increase pathways to obtaining this certification, and districts have started to look at ways to incentivize their current staff to obtain their EL endorsements. Number one, we do want to increase the number of EL-certified staff as our EL student numbers grow. Number two, we want to grow the professional capacity of our current staff so that we're all becoming more skilled and equipped at serving the needs of a growing student group.

There are a few pieces I'd like for us to note. While fast-tracking endorsement courses can increase pathways, we do want to be mindful of implications. A strong endorsement program not only covers the list of required coursework, but it should give educators a solid foundation of knowledge, and also practical application for our work in classrooms and schools. The fast-tracking of endorsement programs can perhaps provide more pathways so more educators have more access to this information, but it could also lessen the actual overall impact that we desire. If the courses are shorter or less rigorous, or they remove the opportunity for dialoguing and reflection, then the impact won't be what our intended outcome was originally. If we're not allowing for deeper levels of knowledge, reflection, and action—all of which should be based on strong and sound theory, solid deeper understandings, actions that we can take in school, and ongoing reflection—then what are we doing? Now folks are walking around with a piece of paper attached to their teaching degrees with a false sense of serving the actual needs of our students.

An educator can have an EL endorsement but not teach with an EL-conscious lens. Similarly, an educator can teach with an EL-conscious lens but not hold a state-approved EL endorsement. We need to be sure that we're equipping educators with the skills and confidence to serve through an EL-conscious lens. The piece of paper, while expensive and time-consuming to achieve, can really just be reduced to just that—a piece of paper—if it is not making the impact our students need.

## Serving Newcomers in Tier 1

One of the biggest questions I tend to get in my inbox or on social media is how to best serve and support newcomer students in tier 1 instruction. Sometimes the question is phrased as, "What should I have my newcomer students do when the rest of my students are working on . . . ?" I understand that this is a complex question with a lot of complex answers and it cannot generally be answered in one email, or even in one phone or Zoom conversation. What I tend to share is that I want us to focus less on providing separate activities for newcomers and instead *prioritize unifying experiences* that are still meaningful for all students. Here are a few examples of unifying experiences that I am referring to:

- ♦ This or That structures
- ♦ Games that have simple structures that don't require language

- Music
- Student-generated design tools (like a listening guide, sketchnote, and/or a WPSQ bank)

## This or That Structures

A This or That structure can be a powerful and linguistically inclusive structure when we talk about serving newcomers and prioritizing a meaningful experience that they can participate in. Using a simple hold-up tool, all students respond to a prompt on the screen and also said aloud by the facilitator/teacher. This tool can be as simple as some Post-Its, a plastic plate with a dry-erase marker, a pinch card (where the two options are displayed and a student would hold up and "pinch" their desired answer), or hand gestures/signals to demonstrate their desired answer. This can be set up as a True/False, a Yes/No, a Real/Fake, a Fact/Fib, or a Correct/Incorrect. These may also be specific content-based choices like Polygon/Not a Polygon, or based on characters or historical figures.

**FIGURE 4.1** A sample of hold-up tools for a This or That structure.
Photograph taken by the author.

I do a lot of these in educator workshops, with some that are just for fun like Crayola Colors: Is this Real or Fake? I'll introduce the topic and ask if there's anyone in the room who feels like they may have some expertise in this area. For example, if we're exploring Taylor Swift song titles, I'll ask if there are any "Swifties" in the room. We'll either partner up or do this individually. Then we get to the prompts. I'll go through a few different song titles that are real, and some that are just ones that I completely made up. I'll flash each one on the screen and say it out loud, and participants will hold up if they think that's a real Taylor Swift song, or if it's fake. After participants hold up their answers, I'll reveal the answer on the screen. In between each of these, we'll get some giggles and some "Yess I got that one!" or some "Oh, that one fooled me completely!" After we go through several of these, we'll pause and discuss how comfortable we were with this activity and also share what we did when we were unsure of an answer. Participants will often share that they felt comfortable participating in this because of how I'd respond to their hold-ups. I'll just quickly scan the room, and repeat some of the options: "okay, cool—I see a few fakes over here. Got it. There are also some Reals represented over here. Cool . . ." and then we go on to reveal the answer and share the next prompt. It felt very low-stakes in that way. I also ask participants what they did when they were unsure of an answer. Most folks will say that they'd look around the room and see what other folks were holding up. Some will share that they'd look over to the resident expert we identified before we started to see which answer they're holding up. Others will share that they'd measure how confident folks were in their answers—"I looked around the room and the people with their hands higher in the air are generally more confident, and when folks don't know the answers they'll hold it lower. I'd pick whatever the more confident folks were saying."

Once this is done, I distribute a listening guide. Now, I understand that some folks would use a listening guide as more of an anticipatory set, where they have students fill this out before we do the hold-up tool experience. However, in this case, when I'm thinking of using this structure as a unifying experience and also

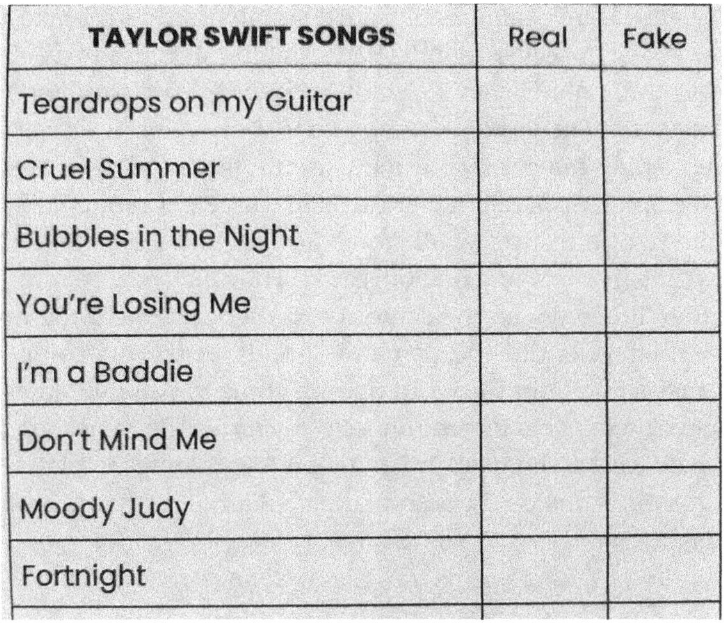

| TAYLOR SWIFT SONGS | Real | Fake |
|---|---|---|
| Teardrops on my Guitar | | |
| Cruel Summer | | |
| Bubbles in the Night | | |
| You're Losing Me | | |
| I'm a Baddie | | |
| Don't Mind Me | | |
| Moody Judy | | |
| Fortnight | | |

**FIGURE 4.2** Sample listening guide that can accompany a This or That structure. This becomes a linguistic scaffold that carries into the next learning experience that can support multiple language domains.

Photograph taken by the author.

as a look-for or listen-for as we move into the next activities, I would offer the listening guide AFTER we did the whole set of prompts together. I would go through each one on the list and review the answers, "Which of these were REAL songs? Which of these were FAKE?" Then I'll have participants draw a line through all the fake ones, because those are no longer relevant to us. Those listening/reading guides remain on the tables for each group to use as language to hold on to as we watch the content video, listen to the lesson, or do the next activities. These guides can then double as a speaking/writing guide, as they have relevant information written down ready to use for students!

## Unifying Games

Another unifying experience that is beneficial to newcomers but can still be meaningful to all students is using the game Spot It.

This game is awesome because it's small and doesn't take up a lot of space in a classroom. They come in all types of versions, too—including a Disney Princess version, MLB teams, and even versions that are based on popular TV shows. There are multiple ways to play the game, but the way my family plays is that we put the small deck of circular cards in the center of the table and we flip two cards up. We all crowd around and we try to find the icons that are matching on both cards. They may be different sizes but they'll always be the same color. Whoever spots the match first either yells out the name, or points to the matching icon (because sometimes the word doesn't come to you that quickly!). Whoever wins gets to keep those two cards. Then we start with two new cards. The game only takes a few minutes to play when you play like this, so it doesn't take up a lot of instructional time.

**FIGURE 4.3** Spot It!
Photograph taken by the author.

This game is wonderful in classrooms because it's linguistically inclusive. Even if you don't know all the words on the cards, you can still participate fully by pointing to the match. I have loved this game so much that I spent endless hours searching for a generator to create your own version—and after a lot of time, I found one! This means that we can create our own versions of this game to play based on the vocabulary of our instructional units, or "survival" vocabulary like words that we use a lot in the classroom (notebook, highlighter, chair, etc.). To do this, you will need to link certain graphics to your vocabulary words. I love websites like The Noun Project or Flat Icon because you can find printer-friendly icons for classroom use that are either black and white or full color. I might even go through these WITH students so that we can accurately capture the words' meaning through dialogue. "Do you think this graphic accurately captures the word *evaporation*? Why or why not?" Having this thoughtful conversation helps students at all proficiency levels to better understand the word and consider how well the graphic represents the idea. Once you link your graphics to your words, you can enhance this by stretching out the word so students see multiple representations of the word (for example: evaporation, evaporates, evaporated, evaporating, etc.). You can also provide synonyms for the word, and show the word in multiple languages. Once you have all of this collected (and have students join you in this process!), you can have students utilize these icons in their reading, writing, listening, and speaking about the words. As students develop their connection between the word and its meaning (along with that graphic representation of the word), you can have them play Spot It using those graphics!

Visit the website https://macrusher.github.io/dobble-generator/ and you'll see right away that you don't even need an account to create this game, which is fantastic! Now, you can simply plug the graphics into the generator and hit the generate button! It'll keep count for you of how many graphics you've uploaded and how many cards you can make. It'll give you prompts that say how many more images to upload if you

| English | Spanish | Image |
|---|---|---|
| altitude | altitud |  |
| atmosphere | atmósfera |  |
| correlation | correlación | |

**FIGURE 4.4** Sample co-constructed vocabulary tool bank.
Photograph taken by the author. Graphics are from Flat Icon.

wanted to create a larger deck of cards (31 cards with 6 images per card is definitely a sweet spot for a nice, healthy deck!). This doesn't mean you have to go back to those websites to find more graphics related to the content—this means now you can add graphics that are just-for-fun. Find your local sports team logos, a picture of your school mascot, your own pets, your principal, your students' favorite characters, and more. Now you've got your full deck of cards to print (I prefer to print these on cardstock), cut, and laminate! You can put these in envelopes for storage, or you can go to your local dollar store and grab circular tins that they have for office supply storage (like little paper clip containers). I found some that are sold in a two-pack and they're also magnetic, so I can just pop them into the container and stick them to my magnetic white board for easy storage! I can label each container with the content area and unit number for easy reference. As we go throughout the school year, I can continue to reinforce vocabulary from previous units by including those graphics into the next unit's set of vocabulary Spot-Its.

Ensuring Equity and Access for Multilingual Learners at Tier One ◆ 111

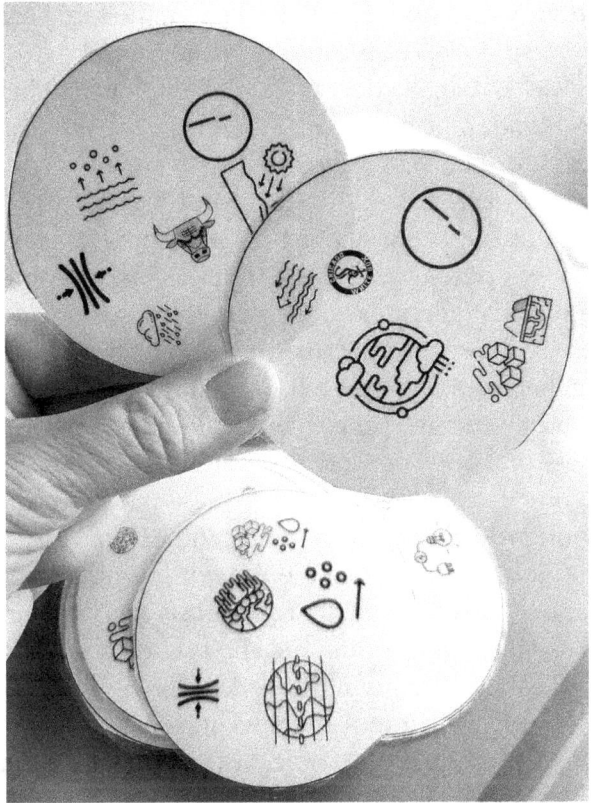

**FIGURE 4.5** Sample content-specific Spot It game created from a generator. The generator can be found at https://macrusher.github.io/dobble-generator/
Photograph taken by the author. Graphics are from Flat Icon.

## Music

Music can serve as a unifying experience for students. Did you know that when folks sing together in a choir, their heartbeats sync up? Wow! Talk about a unifying experience!

I have a lot of music interests across different decades and genres, but I am a huge Beach Boys fan. My own children laugh at me and tell me that's not music from my generation, but it's definitely music from my childhood. Every time I hear Beach Boys music, I think of cruising around with my dad around the city and suburbs as a kid. I think of classic car shows in the summer. I think of being carefree and ice cream and ponytails and sunglasses. Just recently, I had the chance to attend a Beach Boys concert with my husband. He doesn't share the same connection with their music as I do, but he was willing to take me anyway. The concert was at an outdoor venue where you can bring your own chairs, food, and beverages. We packed a few things and headed out.

When we got there, we found a spot and sat for about an hour in the pouring rain, waiting for the show to start. By the time the show started, it stopped raining, and people started to emerge out of their makeshift tents they made to keep dry. We noticed everyone around us for the first time—folks of all ages and generations. The Beach Boys started their set and, hit after hit, I kept dancing "bigger" in my lawn chair. Two women spotted me—probably around my parents' age—and signaled for me to come join them dancing. I threw my food to the floor and ran over and proceeded to dance with these kind strangers for the next hour or so. It was the time of my life! I don't know their names and we didn't exchange stories—we just danced and laughed and high-fived. When the show was over my husband laughed and asked who my new besties were.

We were able to just join together in the shared love of the Beach Boys. It was one of the coolest experiences. And, as a total sidenote, I wish to be like these women, who enjoy life and look around for others to include.

Taylor Swift fans across the world have also bonded over their shared love of her art and music. They exchange friendship bracelets, take selfies with each other, and hype each other up. The fanbase unites over their shared interests and it's actually a really cool thing to observe. Even though I'm not a certified Swiftie, I absolutely respect this woman's impact on her field, her creativity, and her ability to use her voice and platform for issues that matter to her. Music can bring people together.

The same is true for our classrooms. When students have a shared love of something, it can create moments that bond them together. When we talk about serving newcomer students, we can create opportunities for music in the hopes that it can connect students to each other (and maybe to us, too!).

We can get creative with ways to incorporate music into our spaces, too. Whether it's playing music from around the world as students walk into the school in the morning, playing a few instrumental versions of top 40s songs from YouTube while students work, having a "dance party" music break during passing periods, or singing together in class—the possibilities are endless.

During instruction, we can also seek to incorporate music with the help of artificial intelligence. Education websites like MagicSchool AI has a feature called Song Generator where you can type in a song topic, include a few simple details (like perhaps some vocabulary words or key ideas from your unit), and then you can pick a real song title and artist name so that it can generate song lyrics to the tune of your students' favorite songs! Now they can sing about the water cycle to the familiar tune of their favorite Sabrina Carpenter song.

You could take it a step further and use another AI tool called Suno. I was first introduced to this tool from an amazing EL educator, Kimmy Schuelke from Plainfield, IL, who has used this with her elementary multilingual learners. This website, suno.com, will create two original songs for you based on a description box of up to 200 characters. You can include the genre of music, topic, key vocabulary terms to include, class details (like perhaps your class pet or your school mascot), and then hit the button—and in just about 60 seconds, you will have two choices (same lyrics, different melodies and beats). Print out the lyrics for your students, learn the song together, and boom—now you have all bonded over music related to your content!

As an added bonus, you can take the song lyrics and place them side-by-side with a grade-level text in any content area and have students compare the language across the two different genres. Together you can analyze linguistic differences at the word level (word choice and vocabulary), sentence level (grammatical structures and sentence complexity), or at the discourse level (stanzas vs. sentences, repetition and rhythm vs. sentence length, etc.).

## Co-Constructed Tools

Many of us were taught once upon a time that when we serve multilingual learners, there's a lot of planning that we must do in advance. While this can be true (depending on purpose, structure of the activity, etc.), we can also look at how to co-construct tools with our students that can serve everyone in class. When students can co-construct the scaffolds together, there is often a lot of power and opportunity in this. We can model the thinking aloud portion of what we might need to be successful here.

One simple example of this is a Word Phrase Sentence Question (WPSQ) bank. This may be done in the middle of an instructional unit after we've had a few days of learning about the specific topic. We might engage in the co-construction of this with students before starting a lesson or even a video. "Okay, based on what we've been learning, what kind of words are we probably going to hear in the video?" As students share, we simply collect the language of the room. We go across each column asking the same question, "Now what phrases will we probably hear or see today? What full sentences might we hear or use today?" Finally, you can end with the Question column. You could switch this one up in a few different ways by asking students, "What questions might we be able to answer after today?" or "What questions might another 7th grader have

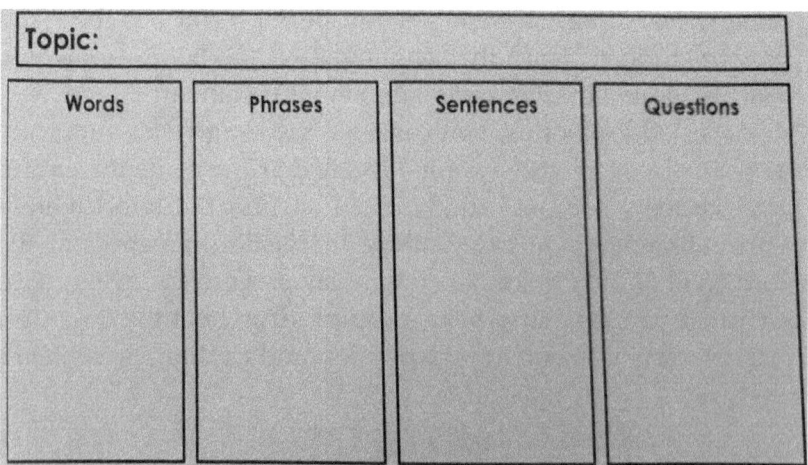

**FIGURE 4.6** Sample of a Word Phrase Sentence Question (WPSQ) chart.
Photograph taken by the author.

about this topic?" You could even come back to this column at the end of class and ask students about what new questions they have, or what questions they might ask the next period of students (if you teach middle or high school). You as the teacher can certainly add to this by asking students, "We've been using this phrase/word a lot. Do you think we should add it here, too?"

You can also revisit this tool after the video or lesson or activity and add more language to it. You might also annotate this tool with students. After the lesson or application, you can ask students to reflect on how they languaged about the content with these words, phrases, sentences, or questions. Perhaps you lead a quick check-in and say, "How many of you used this word or heard this word today?" and keep a tally. "How many of us said this sentence today in our group work time?" You could even add to it by saying, "Now that you've seen the mini lesson / watched the video, what do you think we might add to this?"

What's great about a tool like a WPSQ bank is that it is a tool that can carry. By that, I mean that it is a tool that can be carried into other activities, like group work or independent applied practice. All students now have access to languaging that might be needed to navigate or express ideas about the content. This is not a tool that is reserved for just certain members of the classroom and remains open to everyone.

Utilizing a structure like a speaking/writing guide can empower students to have a specific "look for" or "listen for" as they navigate texts or conversations. This may come in the form of a co-constructed WPSQ bank, or it could come in a checklist or graphic organizer format as well. The earlier example we had with the Taylor Swift songs is a listening guide that students can use to track their thinking and learning. You could also gamify this structure and create a Listening Bingo or Expression Bingo.

When I was in college, I had to take a chemistry class as part of my undergraduate studies. Chemistry was never my biggest passion, but I did okay. On lecture days, I'd hang out an extra while longer in the lobby of the lecture hall, because listening to lectures takes a LOT of stamina, even on days when I'm well rested and feeling good. One day, I noticed a classmate passing out pieces of paper. I assumed it was a flier to a party or event on campus. I walked over and she handed me a piece of paper—it ended up not being a flier at all, but rather a blank bingo board. At the top, she listed out all the quirky languaging that our chemistry professor often used. For example, he would often finish random sentences with "in accordance with the gods." Below that list was a blank bingo card template. The directions on the paper were to pull from the list and plug those into the bingo board. Then, as the lecture unfolded, you'd listen for him to say those words/phrases. If you got a bingo during class, you'd stretch your hands upward real big and snap twice. That way, the professor wouldn't know you got a bingo, but your classmates all knew. It was so fun, and so silly—but to be honest, I was a MUCH better listener on those days. I had an additional PURPOSE for listening!

We can absolutely take this into the classroom by creating a Listening Bingo or a Reading Bingo experience for students, especially as we help them to build stamina for longer stretches of listening or reading. Students at beginning proficiency levels may simply check off the words or phrases as they hear them. Students at higher proficiency levels may annotate the sheet as they hear words/phrases with additional language, heritage language connections, or doodles.

You might also have this as a tool in reverse for students to utilize as they speak or write about content. This might incentivize students to use certain words or phrases in context with their classmates or in their independent writing.

### Translation by Itself Isn't a Scaffold

One piece that I want teachers and leaders to be mindful of is the use of translation and interpretation as a means to provide access to grade-level content. Earlier in Chapter 2 we talked about how important it is to nurture a multilingual ecosystem and elevate the languages of our communities. As we focus this chapter on our instructional practices, we can talk about how to effectively utilize translation and interpretation strategically.

With the onset of artificial intelligence and other technology tools that can provide instant translations, we need to consider how to use these to maximize opportunities for our students. If we show teachers a few new translation features available to us in our curricular resource or on the internet, without setting and identifying purpose and parameters, it can become a slippery slope to practices that don't equitably serve our students.

I've worked with a number of schools that have shown their staff a few different ways to provide heritage language access to content during a workshop, and then classroom, content, and even multilingual teachers will resort to using that as "THE scaffold." I'm here to tell you that this is not a scaffold. Providing a resource in a heritage language alone, especially when the language of instruction is English, is not adequate—and it is not equitable. Many teachers though will see this as a "quick fix" or a band-aid, and solely rely on this.

Relying on translation alone is problematic for a few reasons. First, it assumes a level of literacy skills in a heritage language. If we don't share an additional language with students, measuring a student's abilities in their language can be difficult. Most of us do not have an assessment measure that is an authentic assessment—meaning it was designed in the heritage language first, and not just an English assessment translated into another language. Because of this, we have no real way of assessing a student's literacy abilities in that language. So by providing a 4th grade translation of our English resource into Ukrainian, we are assuming the student has literacy skills at the 4th grade level. How are we to know?

Second, the purpose of providing heritage language links is to provide an entrance ramp into the content—not deliver a full play-by-play of everything that's happening. This means that we don't need to provide a grade-level translation of the content for our newcomer students. If we are teaching with 4th grade level texts and resources, reduce the reading level to a 2nd grade text prior to translating. This allows the overall "gist" to get communicated, and will rely on solid instruction for students to understand the content using additional tools, scaffolds, and supports.

Third, so much gets "lost" in translation. The English language is full of words that have multiple meanings. By using AI or other tech-based translations, those softwares will often just select a meaning on your behalf. For example, if I were to use the word "can" and ask the tech tool to translate it, the tool has no idea if I mean a can of soup, or the verb can like "I can do it!" Furthermore, when a language has multiple dialects, the tech tool usually isn't sophisticated enough to understand the variations in dialect, so they just collect ALL of them and spit them out together. It becomes a linguistic salad that doesn't actually provide any clear meaning.

Interpretation (providing additional language for spoken languaging) also deserves some attention and reflection. When newcomer students begin their first few days in US classrooms, I've heard of folks utilizing their bilingual staff to shadow the newcomer students. This sounds like a good idea to help newcomer students have a smoother transition into their new school with a new language. They'd essentially follow them from class to class and interpret the content all day long. They'd also support the student in explaining the rules and expectations for transitioning to different activities, different classes, explain the layout of the cafeteria, finding your bus at the end of the day, etc. For instructional purposes, we want to leverage our shared language strategically.

First, the first few days of being immersed in a new environment are really overwhelming, and often pretty overstimulating. If you lay an additional language on top of that new environment, the overstimulation is heightened to a new level. If you also lay a third layer of shared language on top of the other layers, it's a whole lot. So, in an effort to remove some of the sense of overwhelm and overstimulation, we must have conversations about how to effectively and strategically utilize interpretation.

I've also seen the multilingual community's response to this overreliance on translation and interpretation. Some folks have come together to design a flow chart of when it might be helpful to utilize translation or interpretation for instructional purposes. I absolutely respect the idea and intention behind this, but reducing educator reflection to just following a flow chart cannot adequately equip teachers with the skills needed to make equity-based decisions for their newcomer students. Instead, I recommend creating a Translation for Instruction Protocol, and also an Interpretation for Instruction Protocol. Translation means providing an additional language for written documents. Interpretation means providing an additional language for spoken language.

All educators must understand the purpose, or the Why, in addition to the How. This is why it's important that a protocol is collaboratively constructed by a group of educators and leaders, and not just created in a room by one person and distributed to others. Professional learning paired with

**TABLE 4.1** Sample Translation Protocol for Instructional Purposes to Support Newcomer Students Using Three Prongs: Strategic, Translation, AND

| | |
|---|---|
| Purpose | Leveraging our students' heritage language affirms their linguistic identity and helps students to access content as a scaffold, especially for newcomer students. Knowing our students' heritage language literacy skills plays a role in this work. When done well, this can be an example of a linguistically and culturally responsive way to nurture more inclusive learning environments. |
| When (**Strategic**) | When considering when to utilize translation, it's important to be strategic. Identify which pieces or parts of instruction might be best used for translation—for example, when giving directions, introducing new vocabulary, or allowing students options to express their learning or understanding. |
| How (**Translation**) | Utilize adult human translators whenever possible. |
| | Enable Auto-Translate CC for YouTube videos (great for shorter videos). Adjust the playbook speed to .75 to allow students the time to read. Allow students the opportunity to view the video twice—once to read the translated text, and once to view the content of the video. |
| | Automatically translate within Canva across your designs (Apps -> Translate -> Select Language) |
| | Use AI translations like DeepL or Diffit to translate text or files. |
| | Use Google Translate to translate text, files, or images. |

*(Continued)*

**TABLE 4.1** (Continued)

| | |
|---|---|
| Cautions | Be cautious of word-to-word translations! There are many words with multiple meanings in English. Many tech tools will pick a definition on your behalf! Utilize synonym groupings to help cut down on "lost in translation" moments. |
| | Be cautious of languages with multiple dialects. Often, Google and AI translators aren't sophisticated enough to translate within dialects, so it generates a mixture of dialects, which may not be comprehensible to students. |
| | Be cautious not to assume a level of heritage language literacy skills of students. When providing a translated set of resources, consider adjusting the reading level prior to generating a translation. Students do not need a grade-level translation of content! By changing the grade level prior to translating, this allows an entry point into the content instead of a direct play-by-play. |
| | Be cautious of vocabulary differences from country to country, even within one language. For example, there are many ways to translate the word *popcorn* into Spanish in different countries. |
| | Be cautious not to lean solely on translation. Identify your *AND*. What else will you be utilizing to make your content more accessible *in addition to* the translation? |

### (AND)

collaborative conversations, including citing specific examples by content area and curricular resources, can lead to a richer and more complete protocol with more understanding to support teachers in decision making. A protocol without understanding is just a piece of paper.

A rich protocol should include the purpose of translation, examples of translations available to the staff along with some practical tips or moments of when specific tools might be used, and some think points. There should also be an explicit call to action for teachers that this is one layer of support that must be used *in addition to* other language supports. Teachers who just stop at translation or interpretation alone are not adequately supporting newcomer students.

The protocol should be collaboratively constructed, shared in teams, and brought back to the teams throughout the school year for ongoing reflection and conversation.

## Serving Students at Higher Proficiencies in Tier 1

There is a huge misconception about serving multilingual learners that we must flood the most intensive supports for students who are newer to their language journey in English, and then we must scale way back as students grow in their proficiency levels. When I say "scale back," I mean next to nothing outside of some type of "EL teacher time"—whether that's a pullout of 30 minutes per day, or 60 minutes per week of in-class support. Classroom and content teachers are told either explicitly or implicitly that the "language learning" is being handled by the EL teacher whereas their job is to teach the content. The truth is that every student, whether or not they are identified as a language learner or multilingual learner by their state, needs support in the language demands of all the various content areas.

There is often the overreliance on the "language support" to come directly from the EL teacher, but what happens when the EL teacher only has 30 minutes a day or 60 minutes a week with the student? Who is supporting the language needs of students when the EL teacher is not in the room? Linguistically supportive instruction is the BARE MINIMUM expectation for BASIC COMPLIANCE of every educator in the school. Period. Let me say again that if we don't provide accessible content in our instruction, we are not meeting the most basic of civil rights of multilingual students.

Sometimes teachers who don't have a solid understanding of language proficiency levels will assume that because students are reading from the textbook, or talking in their small groups, or raising their hands during class, or speaking socially with their friends in the hallways, or writing paragraphs in their notebooks—that this means the students don't need any language support. So they don't offer any language support. Meaning that many times, students at higher proficiency levels don't receive adequate language support at tier 1.

As students grow in their proficiencies, it is important again to note that language has no ceiling. I've been languaging in English for about 40 years (or um, 29 years, I mean, because I'm so very young and hip), and I still don't know ALL the words. Don't ask me to know, or much less utilize, the language of law school, chemistry, or American football. I don't feel comfortable engaging in conversations about Wall Street, or astrophysics, or construction sites. I don't know all regionalisms across the country, and even though I had Southern grandparents, I don't know or understand all of the Southern sayings from my Southern friends or family members. This doesn't mean I'm "bad at" languaging in this language.

This does mean if I'm engaging with content with topics that are new to me, or topics that I'm not interested in or passionate about, or topics that I don't have a lot of experience in, I may need a little more languaging support so that I can access the content and express my ideas about it. So let's talk about how this support might look.

One common piece that gets discussed (and heavily argued about) is leveling texts for students. People on social media—some experts, some not—have gone to great lengths to tell us if this is something we should be doing as teachers or should never touch with a ten-foot pole. Things have gotten so incredibly heated that it feels controversial to even talk about this in some circles!

As a learner myself, I use a variety of text types (genres) and reading levels to learn about unfamiliar topics. Sometimes when the topic is new to me, grabbing an academic journal feels a little intimidating. So I may pair that with a few blogs and social media posts about the topic. I may even go into the comments section of social media posts (ahhh! I'm *such* a risk taker!) to grab some social language to help me unpack the topic. Then maybe I go back to the academic journal to continue to build up my knowledge. I often do this type of information collecting through reading, listening, and viewing various pieces of content. After I get a few different passes through the content in this way, I feel a little more equipped to have conversations with folks about the topic.

How do you tend to learn about topics that are unfamiliar to you?

I don't think that providing a leveled text (purposefully and intentionally throughout a unit) is the terrible thing we're made to believe. I do, however, wholeheartedly note that by ONLY providing students with leveled texts (especially when they are below grade-level texts) we are creating equity gaps. Students (and I mean ALL students, not just multilingual students) should have a variety of text levels and genres to pull from as they build up their content skills and knowledge.

If we scan across the course of our instructional week, we might consider when a leveled text might be appropriate. We also might consider when grade-level text is used. We also likely consider additional resources and materials that are presented across different genres (video, images, stories, anecdotes, examples, lists, infographics, interviews, posters, etc.) that can assist in understanding the topic.

Leveled texts, when used exclusively, absolutely strip students of the opportunity to read, navigate, consume, and interpret more complex language (through different word choices and vocabulary, grammatical structures, and language choices that denote mood and tone, for example). If a student uses a leveled text at any point, we must identify when students have the opportunity to read grade level texts.

One missing piece of all of this is having students develop their metalanguaging skills (their ability to think about their languaging) by propping those two texts side by side. The human brain actually loves doing this. Do you remember Highlights magazine and those Spot the Difference pictures in the back? We LOVED that stuff! Adults continue to do this by looking at Before and After moments. Think of all the beauty makeover shows in the 90s (or the late 1900s, as my own kids call it—insert side eye here). Weren't they problematic?! Anyway, those sort of faded out as shows but those Before and After moments are still alive and well on Instagram ads that promote under-eye color correctors. We also have an entire television network devoted to home makeovers, like the shows that "flip" a house (and gentrify neighborhoods) and share the Before photos next to the After photos. We eat that stuff up!

In short, if our brains enjoy that sort of thing, how can we use this in our instruction?

When students have the opportunity to explore two texts side by side and analyze them, compare them, and consider the texts through different lenses, their languaging is expanded. Now students can see how a thought is expressed within one genre or within specific phrasing, and compare it to the expression in a different genre or different phrasing. This builds up their bank!

Of importance to note, by arranging the two language samples side by side, it doesn't physically "prioritize" or "elevate" one type of text over the other. One is not "on top of" or more significant than the other. More on this in a moment.

I love to use a side-by-side structure when utilizing leveled texts and making notes and comparisons. It can serve as a scaffold for students at beginning proficiency levels, and can also serve as a language stretcher for students at higher proficiency levels.

We can also use a side-by-side structure by comparing across genres. For example, students can engage by looking at how our textbook represented civil rights protests of the 1960s, compared to lyrics of protest songs. While both are expressing similar ideas, the structure of the expression is quite different.

Using side-by-side structures doesn't mean that we'd ALWAYS put a grade level text side-by-side with a leveled text, but we should identify a few times throughout the unit (or the week) where we take samples of the texts that we use and have conversations about the different ways to represent the ideas using different language choices.

## The Positioning of "Academic Language"

Textbook companies and assessment companies (and sometimes they are one and the same, which is—oh, yes—incredibly problematic) love to tell us folks in education that academic language is superior to social or informal language. They tell us that to be "college and career ready" we must be able to access and utilize academic language. They want us to tell our students that social language is less valuable. This messaging that gets created and passed down reinforces linguistic hierarchies inside of our classrooms.

If I tell my students that it is "better" to use the word "rotate" instead of "spin" because that's what our textbook says, or that is the language of the test, then I am upholding linguistic hierarchies. If I instead tell students that both pieces of language are important and both have value, we can be empowered to use both to express ideas to communicate with those around us. Additionally, if I tell my students to "speak like a scientist" but I'm also working diligently to ensure that my students see themselves (and others who don't look like them!) as scientists, then telling them that scientists only speak one type of way might be confusing. Scientists use both "academic" and also "social" languaging because they're human beings.

The solution here is to introduce and leverage a variety of languaging that matches purpose, role, and audience. For example, if I am asking students to explain how to solve our current math problem as if they were explaining it as a teacher to a kindergarten class, we might use specific language choices like, "Hi friends! Let's look at how we can solve tricky problems!" However, if I am asking students to explain how to solve our current math problem as if they were explaining it as a professor at a university, we might use language choices like, "Let's begin by first isolating the unknown factor in the equation." The language choices would match our role and our audience, all for a specific purpose. In both cases, the purpose was explaining how to solve a math problem. I altered the role and audience, which influenced the language choices I was using.

Having reflective conversations with students about language choice helps all of us to extend our languaging powers, and also helps us to develop a more critical eye on languaging expectations based on role and identity.

Additionally, we can take this a whole step further and analyze the WHY behind ALL of this! WHY might we expect a professor at a university to language a certain way? How/why does this look different than chatting with a friend at a coffee shop? Can/does that university professor ALSO language socially with a friend at a coffee shop?

## Measuring Speaking: Imagine This . . .

Humor me, friends. Let's all drift into this imaginative sequence for a bit . . .

If you were to ask me for a speaking sample, I may or may not want to provide one, unless you told me specifically about what I needed to talk about. If you were to ask me to talk about the rules of American football, I honestly wouldn't have a whole lot to tell you. I do know some words in isolation, like touchdown, quarterback, defense, offense, helmet, and yards. I also know a few phrases like *loss of yards, end zone*, and *throw the flag!* You might be surprised that I couldn't explain all of these things to you in detail after cheering in high school and college, and the amount of Chicago Bears games that I watched with my dad growing up in the 80s and 90s, or the amount of times I watched my son play football on various teams throughout his life. If you asked me a few specific questions about football and recorded my answers, and then assessed my ability to speak English using a rubric, you might assign me a score that doesn't accurately reflect my actual speaking abilities.

However, if you asked me to speak for a little bit about serving and supporting multilingual students in classrooms,

I'd happily oblige! I could share details of studies, share ways of how to embrace a multilingual ecology, review instructional strategies, and much more! My own personal interest combined with my experience and expertise would equip me with much more to say.

So let's say I record myself talking about American football, and this recording goes off to someone in an office somewhere who I've never met. They don't know anything about me or my language skills or my language journey. All they know is their speaking rubric and what I've provided in my sample. They are going to take that language in isolation and rate me. Then they'll do the same for all my peers. They eventually send it back to my workplace or organization with a score. This score gets shared with my parents/family/guardians. My boss uses it to make a plan for how to improve my performance. I sure hope my boss takes into consideration all the other elements of my work when trying to evaluate who I am as a languager! My boss sure hopes the organization isn't completely judged by the public eye simply by how well I shared information about American football!

This goes on for years. My boss gets frustrated with me and starts to assume I'm lazy or unmotivated. One time she met my mom and she told her that. I was humiliated because my mom thought I languaged so well! No matter how I continue to work or perform in other areas, this speaking sample I do once a year really weighs on how she views me. She starts to assume that I need a work plan through our HR department to improve. Now I have to complete additional tasks that are devoid of joy, creativity, or higher level thinking—all in the name of improving my speaking ability. I don't get to do the same work as my colleagues and teammates. I start to not like my workplace. I start to disengage. I start to "coast." Some of my colleagues have been overheard saying that "Carly is quiet-quitting," meaning that I just don't try anymore.

There are days that I question my own abilities. There are days that I am just sitting back knowing that no matter what I do, it's not going to make a difference to how my boss or colleagues view me, and it's definitely not going to change my work experience, or afford me any different opportunities.

Every year, my boss asks me for another speaking sample. Year after year, I look forward to this task less and less. In fact, I start to dread it completely. Plus, it takes hours for me to complete. I wish they could just capture my regular conversations. I wish they could hear how excited I get when I talk about things that I love! I wish they could listen as I told stories of my childhood or tales of my own two kids growing up before my very eyes. I wish I could record a piece about a specific skill I have or a topic I know a lot about. I wish I didn't have to submit this stupid sample.

The folks in my organization agree that this feels a little silly to have to do every year, because they've told me before that they know how I can speak. They've told me I communicate just fine! They won't remove me from my boring tasks that I have to complete every day at work and they know I just want to be with my teammates doing the work that excites us. They try to cheer me up with a pizza party every year to get me "hyped up" to submit my sample again. It's nice, but it doesn't eliminate the task I have to complete, or all my feelings associated with it. I eat my slice of pizza, and I record my sample again. In just 12 short weeks, I find out again that the person in an office far, far away still doesn't think my languaging is good enough. Maybe the pizza slice I eat next year will do the trick?

## Okay, We're Back

Reader, do you see what I did there? Let's go back and reread that whole previous section and draw parallels to our students.

That's all. That's the section.

## Speaking Assessments

Okay reader, the little story sequence is over, but you saw the picture being painted, right? Sometimes a speaking assessment is problematic . . .

- . . . especially if a student's speaking score is impacting their learning opportunities.
- . . . especially if it impacts how a student views themselves as a languager.
- . . . especially if students have disengaged from the assessment because of how it has continued to make them feel year after year.
- . . . especially if this is the only measure a teacher (or school system) has to measure a student's speaking growth.
- . . . especially if teachers are not providing adequate speaking time (with effective support) during tier 1 instruction across content areas.
- . . . especially if I am taking the speaking assessment in front of my peers and I'm uncomfortable having an "audience" (or even a "perceived" audience).
- . . . especially if I think this assessment is dumb.

We have to look at what other pieces of information we have that help us paint a more complete picture of our students' abilities and capacities.

## Let's Go!

By starting with tier 1 instruction, we can all collectively focus on the language of our various content areas. By remembering that every single student is growing in language, we can shift our language support from being a part of The After Slap effect and instead being something we start with for everyone. When we prioritize unifying experiences at the instructional level, we can shift from "alternate activities" to meaningful learning experiences for everyone. Engaging in ongoing, high-quality professional learning experiences can help all of us improve our practices. Through these things, we can continue to Question, Equip, and Act so that we all better serve multilingual students across content areas from day one at tier 1!

Let's go! Let's Ignite Real Change!

**TABLE 4.2** Question, Equip, Act (Chapter 4)

| Question | Equip | Act |
|---|---|---|
| What does a linguistically inclusive tier 1 look like and sound like to me? | Investigate structures that you're currently using with your students that are "unifying experiences." Identify the pieces that make it feel unifying. | Pick a block of your instructional time and see how many minutes students are actively engaged in speaking about the content. Reflect on any noticings and wonderings. Share with a colleague. |
| Why might I (or my colleagues) feel uncomfortable supporting students who are new to their language journey in English? What support might I/they need? | Explore your students' language data across reading, writing, listening, and speaking. If you have historical data, go through those scores from year to year. | Play with different instructional structures that allow multiple entry points for all students. When it doesn't go well, revamp it. When it goes well, use it again and share it with colleagues. |
| Have you seen examples of leaning too much on "alternative activities" for newcomer students? Why do you think that is? | Explore your students' speaking scores on annual language assessments. Have conversations with your colleagues about noticings and wonderings. | Collect anonymous feedback from your students about how accessible your teaching is. Get ready to listen and believe your students, and be ready to act on their feedback. |
| Have I witnessed specific examples of The After Slap effect? When/where? | Pick a block of your instructional time and see how many minutes students are actively engaged in speaking about the content. Reflect on any noticings and wonderings. Share with a colleague. | Collaborate with colleagues while planning for instruction and identify entrance ramps and accessibility to various proficiency levels. |
| What are you comfortable speaking a lot about? What are you uncomfortable speaking about? What might you need to feel safer to speak about unfamiliar topics? What might students need? | | Identify an annual day/space for the entire school staff to review language data all together. |

# 5
# Interrupting Inequitable MTSS Tiered Interventions and "Problem-Solving" Structures

"Wow, Carly. All your kids are in the red. You must feel so overwhelmed!"

One of my teammates was reflecting with me the day after one of our data meetings, where all the classroom teachers and specialists came together to review benchmark scores. Just like the story I shared in Chapter 1, my multilingual students were being assessed in just one of their languages, even though it didn't match the language of instruction.

"Nope. My kids are doing great, actually. They overwhelm me with their brilliance every day!"

As the years went on, these conversations irked me more and more. I started fighting this narrative that multilingual students are all "in the red" every chance I got.

## Multilingual Services

One thing we all must understand before we go into this chapter is that multilingual learner services are NOT an intervention. Multilingual learner services are a part of a full continuum that includes intentional and holistic academic and social-emotional supports delivered and supported by every adult in the school ecosystem.

This is where a large number of districts have their wheels fall apart in terms of equity for multilingual students.

Students who are multilingual learners are often some of the most overly assessed students in the school system. This includes all the regular classroom-based and district-based assessments. This includes all of the additional state-regulated assessments. This includes the federally mandated annual language assessment. When multilingual learners are enrolled in a bilingual or dual language program as part of their language services, they are frequently assessed TWICE in one or more of these assessments—once in English and once in the additional language of instruction.

The annual language assessment alone is incredibly time-intensive. Only a few members of staff are typically trained and certified to administer that assessment, which means that several WEEKS of instruction and support are typically interrupted until that assessment window closes. This, alone, is a gigantic red flag. Even if your school or district has a smaller number of students identified as multilingual learners, you should not have just one adult who is certified to administer language tests. We need to minimize the instructional impact on multilingual learners.

What we must reiterate to all teachers and leaders is that a strong tier 1 is often overlooked. Seriously. We often spend so much time putting students into little triangles, categories, and spreadsheets. Let's pretend our jazzy little triangles didn't exist. What would you do? How would you support every student in your class? What professional learning needs might you have? Sometimes folks have become so accustomed to sending kids out of class to be plugged into computers or box programs that we forget that we actually have the responsibility to have a strong tier 1 that is accessible to every student.

Sorting students around into tiers can give teachers a false sense of responsibility, or unintentional permission to abdicate responsibility. If we start our triannual sorting system and determine that a student needs to be on a tier 2 or tier 3 listing, and we place that student's name under an interventionist or on a list of students for various small groups, what message does that send to the classroom teacher? I can't tell you the amount of times I have heard classroom teachers say, "Well at least now that student is getting tiered supports. They're finally going to get their needs met." I'm sorry—WHAT?! "THROW THE FLAG!" Do you mean that if your student wasn't removed from your class for 30 minutes to work somewhere else with someone else that you wouldn't meet their needs when they're with you?

## Assessment Measures

First, what are we using to "benchmark" our students in order to "cast the net?" Most schools do this during the fall, winter, and spring to identify learners who might need additional support. We create these nifty little flow charts to help us in our decision making about which kids might need a "tier 2" or "tier 3" level of support in either literacy or math.

Some of the literacy assessments are especially problematic because they assume that everyone taking the assessment is a monolingual English languager in our classrooms. And we know that's a pretty wild assumption. They have us ask students whose heritage languages don't have the /sh/ sound to correctly read it and say it and then when they don't, we remove points, their scores drop, and they pop up in red on a spreadsheet to indicate that they need intensive intervention.

It's frustrating to hear folks say, "Well, a little extra reading help isn't going to hurt them!" This comment makes me super itchy. If the "little extra reading help" is from a box program that wasn't designed for them (and definitely normed for them), and the person delivering the "little extra reading help" is neither EL-certified nor EL-conscious, then the "little extra reading help" MIGHT NOT HELP AT ALL.

When did we all become so conditioned to believe that a box program (often marketed as "THE solution") is going to "fix" everything for every student? This flawed ideology has harmed multilingual learners for years. Remember, these are often the same folks with the brilliant minds that came up with, *"Here's how to tweak this for your multilingual students: JUST ADD VISUALS! WOOHOO!"* Seriously. It's the same After Slap effect but now it's thrown into tiers (or maybe *tears*?). And yet, these are the same materials that we place our multilingual students into and wait for the "fix" to occur.

Now let's talk about some of the components of these box programs. Some of them feature word lists—words in isolation—words with no context. Meaning, just random word lists. So fun—so engaging (*insert eye roll here*). Or worse—sometimes it's just random sounds in isolation. If you scroll TikTok for a few minutes and search #EnglishIsHard, you might get a bunch of videos that use humor to illustrate this point. There is a creator named @itsbobbyfin who has a series of these types of videos where he does "English class." He'll go through a few words as a teacher (him) with a "student" (which is him in another shirt) and ask the student to read them. For example, he'll write THOUGH on the whiteboard and ask the student to read it. The student will read it correctly and then he'll erase the TH and write a C to make the word "COUGH" and ask the student, "Okay, now what does this word say?" The student will pronounce the word like /co/ to which the teacher will say, "NO! It's COUGH." He'll underline the C and say, "You don't see how . . . I changed it to a C so it changes how you say the rest of the word!" The student will get visibly frustrated. The teacher will repeat this process with other words like THROUGH, ENOUGH, and TOUGH.

The videos themselves are hilarious because they showcase the absolute absurdity of English "rules." The comments in these videos are equally noteworthy because folks share their own experiences of trying to learn the English language and being taught "rules" in school. It's hard to learn the rules of a language when there are so many annoying irregularities. If adults and kids alike struggle with all of these variations, it is no surprise that English is such a difficult language to learn.

Our own language's proximity to English is also important to note here. If my heritage language is similar-ish to English (meaning we have the same reading system from left to right, and we use the same alphabet), it *might* make the process of learning English go smoother. On the flipside, if my heritage language alphabet is completely different or our reading system is different, it might make my journey into English more difficult.

Many of these "tier 3" intensive literacy programs are scripted. Here's where our (not) favorite f-word comes into play: fidelity. Teachers who deliver this scripted program must read the script for up to 60 minutes of instruction that drills letter sounds, blend sounds, digraph sounds, etc. As an adult, if I was forced to "learn" by having someone read a script to me for 60 minutes every day, I would cry. I would completely disengage. It would destroy my sense of confidence in myself. If this was my reality every single day, school would feel lifeless. Instruction might feel like it is devoid of creativity, higher level thinking, and opportunity to talk and collaborate with my peers. Remember, this is all my perceptions *as an adult*. What if I was 8? What if I was 12?

What I see happen in schools is that we put kids into spreadsheets after completing a "baseline sweep." We identify certain scores or percentages we'd deem as needing some tier 2 support. We identify certain scores or percentages we'd deem as needing tier 3 support. Then we plug those kids into spreadsheets. We don't have conversations about each of the students on those spreadsheets.

If we do that sweep and sort and don't have conversations, we are going to find that a lot of students who are still acquiring English are going to be present on those spreadsheets for needing either tier 2 or tier 3 services. If we were to gather all of the tiered lists, what percentage of each tier are multilingual students? What does that tell us about the appropriateness of the assessment? Does it make sense for them to take that assessment to begin with?

Your school's sweep and sort must include ALL data, including language data. If the student is still developing in language, is it appropriate to not only use the same sweeping measure but weigh it the same as monolingual students who are "proficient" in the language? If your spreadsheets don't include language levels, this is one small thing to start doing right away. Don't just include an overall composite score, but include individual language domain scores (reading, writing, listening, speaking) and other composited scores like literacy, oracy, and comprehension. This allows us to consider the student's needs and determine if they still need more instructional time with more high-quality tier 1 instruction before being plugged into a tier 2 or tier 3 program.

I used to work with a district where we'd include this data, review it, and then determine if we needed to "beef up" and enhance tier 1. The truth is, all tier 1 instruction MUST BE BEEFED UP AND ENHANCED LINGUISTICALLY. Otherwise, your tier 1 is weak and inequitable by definition. And yes, let's revisit—whose responsibility is it to make tier 1 linguistically enhanced and supportive? That's right—EVERYONE'S! Not just the multilingual teacher!

## Voices from the Field

### Jennifer Frankowiak, K-5 ELD/Newcomer Teacher, Sheiko Elementary, West Bloomfield Schools

In my years as a teacher of multilingual students I'm always making sure that each one of my multilinguals is able to have equal access to the curriculum. A few years ago I had a student who was struggling in his 3rd grade classroom right after the pandemic. Some colleagues were quick to feel he should be evaluated for special education. As his ELD teacher I had to advocate for him over the next three years. When he first entered my classroom he was discouraged and felt like he couldn't do anything. Over the next three years I continued to advocate for him. By the middle of 4th grade he finally told me he saw himself as a reader and kept thanking me and the reading tutor he had. In three years with help from

> another colleague and an amazing 5th grade classroom teacher he was finally able to see himself as a learner and grew to almost being on grade level. He is now in middle school and getting all A's in his classes. Every time I see him he gives me a big bear hug and it makes me feel like I made a difference in his life. I will always advocate for my multilingual students to ensure they are getting the best education to be successful.

This means that we might determine that a multilingual learner does not receive tier 2 or tier 3 interventions. This means that we might determine that a multilingual learner should remain in the content classrooms with supportive tier 1 instruction that provides access to grade level content.

This might mean that we do provide a tier 2 or tier 3 intervention. If this is the case, we must work diligently to ensure that whatever the intervention is includes linguistically enhanced tiered instruction, the curricular materials being used have been designed and normed for multilingual learners, the progress monitoring measures are linguistically appropriate, and the intervention is delivered by someone who is BOTH EL-Endorsed AND ALSO EL-Conscious. If you can't check all these boxes, then your tiered supports are not equitable for the multilingual learners you serve.

## Voices from the Field

### Dr. Denise Furlong, Author of Voices of Newcomers

> I used to work in a school in which learners who receive ESL services were automatically excluded from other supports such as basic skills or

> intervention services. It was considered "double dipping" as they incorrectly categorized ESL services as a separate form of intervention. (*Note: ESL is not intervention!*) A different school did not permit multilingual learners to receive interventions because none of the interventionists spoke their heritage languages and they felt it would be a waste of everyone's time. Over many years and several schools, I found that sometimes educational systems spent more time excluding multilinguals from potentially beneficial programs than simply providing those services.

## Data Analysis Through the Multilingual Learner Lens

Historical language data is also a hugely important piece of this conversation. We must look historically at how students have grown each year in each domain of language. Our collective data literacy must be strong. We must understand how to analyze language data for our state's language assessment. When I say "we" I mean the full data team—meaning whoever is around that table making decisions about student services and tiered placements. This probably includes principals, coordinators, interventionists, classroom teachers, school psychologists, and other specialists.

All states are required to have an annual language assessment for students who are identified as multilingual learners. There are, as of this writing, 42 states in the US that belong to the WIDA Consortium, and thus they utilize WIDA's ACCESS test. Other states may have a different annual language assessment. As I work with schools and districts across Illinois and beyond, I think there is a lot of misunderstanding, misinterpretation, and misapplication of ACCESS language data, which makes me wonder if other language assessment users might also be misinterpreting or misusing some of their language data that are specific to their states and assessments. Sometimes leaders will assume that the multilingual learner teacher is fully versed in this area, but these teachers are often not provided with professional learning opportunities (or even provided the time that is required to explore the tools and resources for each assessment) to support the full understanding of how to utilize and interpret this data.

As a quick example, educators often misinterpret the use of a three-digit scale score provided by WIDA and the decimal proficiency level score. The scale scores are meant to be utilized to track linguistic growth from year to year within each individual domain. The proficiency level scores are meant to be utilized as data that informs instruction. There are descriptors for each proficiency level at each language domain that help educators understand what students can do at the end of the proficiency level when instruction is scaffolded appropriately. What I see many times in teams is that they've been measuring student growth from year to year by using proficiency (decimal) scores instead of scale scores. This is an incorrect usage of the data. Again, not shaming anyone here! A lot of us haven't had time to research or we haven't had professional learning experiences that have supported us in understanding this!

We also sometimes forget that our annual language assessment data is not the only language data we have. In fact, in every content area, our students are expressing their learning through speaking, writing, and representing. All year long, our students are generating artifacts that we can use to collect, analyze, and track language growth. It is important to note that this does not mean that we are administering additional assessments. NOPE! We are utilizing what our students are already doing in their content area classes. Perhaps we just grab one piece of writing or speaking about science each month (like a written up lab report, a written journal reflection, a video of them explaining the steps they took to complete the STEM challenge, etc.) and we lay a linguistically based writing rubric on top of it. Boom. Look at us—leveraging content-based linguistic captures of our kids.

I would suggest that the multilingual learner teachers have an annual data retreat to meet with each other to build up and refresh our understanding of all of the data that we can and should utilize to check for student progress and growth, student achievement, and systemic performance at each school building. See Table 5.1 for some examples of data points and considerations the multilingual data retreat might examine.

After each of these annual data retreats, leaders (alongside the multilingual learner teachers, if they are willing and have the capacity/bandwidth) should be sharing this data back to the entire school staff so that we are all held accountable for meeting the needs of all multilingual students.

If we implement this as an (at least) annual part of our school calendar, we can build the capacity of the multilingual department and leadership teams in interpreting and utilizing language

**TABLE 5.1** Potential Questions for Multilingual Data Retreat

| | |
|---|---|
| How are individual students growing in their language development? | Factor in the students' program history, service delivery history, instructional support, linguistic growth by domain each year, and the number of years in US schools and/or years of English language instruction |
| How are individual students achieving grade level success? | Factor in report card grades, progress report grades |
| How are our grade levels supporting multilingual learners in each content area? | Factor in curricular resources, lesson plan design, unit plan design, and opportunities to language about content |
| How are our multilingual learners' needs being met in fine arts, PE, and consumer sciences? | Analyze performance data of multilingual learners in each class compared to monolingual peers, factor in curricular resources, lesson plan design, unit plan design, and opportunities to language about content |
| How are our multilingual learners being represented on teams, clubs, and other extracurricular opportunities? | Examine rosters of each, document specific examples of strong or weak culture and climate of each group—factor in student perceptions of each group |
| Dedicated time for "other" reflections that didn't get discussed yet | |
| Dedicated time for identifying any next steps, takeaways that we will share, date for when we can reconvene as a team to share progress | |

data and other measures to monitor growth, achievement, and monitor our established desired equitable outcomes. Then, when we go to have trimester-based conversations, the team will have richer dialogues that can influence how we support our students (starting at tier 1 certainly, but also how we support students across all tiers).

## Flowcharts Aren't Magical

After we "cast our nets" and do our full benchmark-collecting sweep, we'll sometimes try to just grab data points and make a rule that if a student scores below this number, this means they'll get a tier 2 this or that. We'll create nifty little flowcharts with little text boxes and arrows that describe our process. How fun! But do these cute little flow charts help us remember that we're actually talking about children and not test scores? We cannot be satisfied and stop at a cute flowchart, because the human children we're actually talking about are far more complex creatures than their one little data point.

A flowchart oversimplifies the complex process of instructional planning and programmatic decision making for students. It also leaves many of our multilingual learners inappropriately placed into services that are going to cause harm. I'm not saying that all the hours you spent in creating your flow chart are wasted, but I want you to look at them and see if you have ANYTHING in there about how multilingual learners are viewed through a linguistically responsive lens. How might you enhance your flowchart? Might you add some language to your flowchart that includes linguistic data or amount of time in a linguistically rich and supportive tier 1?

If the purpose of the flowchart is to give guidance for monolingual kids who have all had access to the same exact rich tier 1 learning experiences and all the same amounts of privilege, it sounds like maybe that's a cool starting point. However, I don't know a whole lot of schools with a completely homogenous population. An overreliance of a system (or teams of teachers) on the flowchart diminishes the opportunity for rich conversations that can help us to better understand our students, and also rich dialogues that can help us to ask each other better questions and build teacher and leader capacity of our own data literacies, our own instructional practices, and our own data-based decision making.

A flowchart without conversations and guided team-based decision making is educational malpractice.

## Progress Monitoring and Inappropriate Assessment Measures

If we have multilingual learners who have been determined to need a linguistically and culturally appropriate and responsive intervention, then we must next determine what data is necessary to collect that is also linguistically and culturally appropriate and responsive as we "progress monitor." Within the RTI (response to intervention) and MTSS (multi-tiered systems of support) world, we have typically been taught that students who are in a tier 2 intervention should be monitored or assessed with some measure every two weeks, and students in a tier 3 intervention should be monitored or assessed with some measure every week. This is, friends, a whole lot of assessing. If it's quick and non-disruptive and we'd do it anyway, groovy. If it's time-intensive, doesn't give accurate data that takes into account the students' language ability, or feels painful for the students—then let's reexamine. I've had folks tell me, "Carly, this assessment measure is fine for progress monitoring because it's not time-intensive. It'll only take about two minutes for me to do it with each student!" So, in this case, let's consider the overall impact. If I have to administer this individually to multiple students within a certain stretch of time—how much instructional time is being spent in order to "progress monitor?" Do I have other measures that might give me this information so that I don't have to give my students an additional assessment?

Now, I will also acknowledge that sometimes, seeing weekly progress on something can be a booster for students, particularly if there is positive progress! Woohoo! That's excellent.

However, it's hard to measure language growth from one week to the next. And again, might there be other measures that could give us this without burdening students with the additional assessment?

Let's consider a common tier 2 progress monitoring tool for reading fluency, which is a timed reading passage. My own ability to read "with fluency," as an English languaging adult, is greatly impacted by the topic of the text, my exposure and experience with the topic including my background knowledge, the genre of the passage, and the word choice/vocabulary of the passage. If I was asked to read a non-fiction text about the history of US football, I'd probably read it at a slower rate because I'd be pausing for a lot of unfamiliar words and phrases. Even within a familiar topic for me that I have a level of expertise in (let's say education for multilingual learners), if you asked me to read a research journal that shares statistical data and the results of longitudinal studies, I might read that particular text at a slower rate than a narrative-style blog post. For genre alone, if you were to time how fast I could read the dictionary, you'd likely be alarmed at my "reading level." In general, I'm not a fan of timed reading passages as a progress monitoring tool to measure reading fluency for multilingual learners.

## Culturally Biased Assessments

I'll also note that many of the timed reading passages are laced with cultural bias. For example, many of the passages that my multilingual learners had to utilize referred to assumed "common experiences" of kids in the US, like skiing down a mountain (wait, what?!), or going to the apple orchard in the fall to pick apples (Mrs. Spina, I just go to Target to buy apples!), or visiting the local zoo or aquarium. The students who may have had these experiences no doubt outperformed (or outread) the students who did not have these experiences.

The passage about skiing down a mountain has still stuck with me to this day. Yes—this was an actual example of a 3rd grade reading passage that I was supposed to use with my students. I myself have never gone skiing. I still don't really have the interest to ski as an adult (not to mention how accident-prone I am and how I already have issues with my tailbone and hips). I grew up as a kid on the north side of Chicago. If you're unfamiliar with the geography of northern Illinois, we don't have mountains. In the city itself, we don't really even have hills. Folks outside of the city that I've met in life were surprised to know that as a kid, I never even went *sledding* (let alone skiing), because we didn't have nearby sledding hills. The way the kids in my neighborhood "went sledding" is that we'd pack our front steps (yes, our stairs to the front door) with snow on one side of the stairs, and leave the other side of the stairs as steps to climb up. After hours of work, we'd start to "sled" by sliding our butts down the stairs. We'd only get a few passes down our makeshift hill before having to repack the snow so that it didn't hurt our butts and backs too much (new revelation—perhaps this began the issues with tailbone and hips?). Then we'd have to spend hours removing the snow when we were done so we didn't accidentally harm our family members who needed to use the stairs to enter and exit our homes.

Perhaps you're reading this and thinking what resourceful and creative children we were. And YES—we were. Thank you so much for noticing. Or perhaps you're reading this and thinking that you just cannot imagine a childhood without sledding. Well, if that's you—buckle up friend, because there's a lot more assumed experiences than we realize!

Can we also just address how freaking expensive it is to go skiing? First, I'd have to be able to drive us or transport us to a skiing place. Look at me—I still don't have the background knowledge and experience to know what a "skiing place" is called. Is it a skiing lodge? A skiing resort? Doesn't "a resort" mean there's a hotel, too? I digress. Then, I'd have to have all the ski stuff. Ski stuff, like you know, the skis. And I think people who ski wear goggles. And I don't know, maybe elbow pads and knee pads and stuff? Definitely a snow suit. Are there special ski shoes or boots that you wear that get hooked into the skis? Who knows. That sounds expensive already. Perhaps you rent this stuff, but that still sounds pricey. Then you have to pay for your skiing tickets, probably. Perhaps there's like a skiing pass that gets you "in" to whatever the local mountain is that you hurl yourself down. I bet there's people who even pay extra money to get special skiing lessons. So is this a rich sport? A sport for the elite? An activity for the privileged? I truly and honestly 100% have no idea!

What are some of the other assumed childhood experiences that textbook companies write about with such enthusiasm? I shared one of my own examples and I was a kid who grew up with LOTS of privilege in life (including white privilege, language privilege, socioeconomic/middle class privilege, etc.). Just imagine if we were to even dip our toes into exploring the actual lived experiences of our students who come to us from all over the world. But no, those don't make it into the curricular resource think tanks. You might ask, "well, why is that?" The answer lies in WHO is at the curricular resource think tanks. Which privileged folks are there writing on behalf of all of our students?

## Problem-Solving Conversations

Now let's shift our focus and go on to talk about what happens after a student goes through a few rounds of tier 2 or tier 3 interventions and is not making any growth or progress. We've already ensured that each stage of the game thus far has been linguistically and culturally appropriate and responsive, right? Great. So now that we haven't seen any growth (using appropriate and responsive measures), we bring a team of folks together around the table to have a conversation. Many of our schools and districts call this a "problem-solving" meeting.

We walk around saying "This kid needs to be brought up for Problem Solving" or we say "We'll finally get to the bottom of this at Problem Solving." We use the term to indicate a verb, an event, and/or a place. To be honest, everytime I hear it, it makes me itchy. Yes—I itch a lot. Unfortunately there's no ointment or medication to all my inequity-based itchiness, at least not that I've found yet. I'll keep you posted.

To be completely honest, I've also used this term ("problem solving") in my conversations over the years. I've used it as a verb, an event, and a place. But it still haunts me as being a little (or a lot) problematic.

First, can I ask WHAT we're calling a problem? And are we to assume that we around the table are the ultimate SOLVERS of "THE PROBLEM?" Weird that parents, guardians, and the grownups of students are often completely ignored in this particular part of the conversation. What if we reframed the phrase and called it something else—but what? Might we call it A Conversation Table? Might we call it a Supportive Dialogue? Might we call it a Student Support Summit? Any of those sound pretty cool. I just hate the idea of calling it a "Problem-Solving Meeting." A lot of these meetings tend to make the adults around the table create a list of all the things a student can't do yet. Then we make another list of all the things one adult (alone) at the table has to do to "fix" the problem. It's a weird vibe. A lot of our systems have been using this as a structure for decades. Yikes!

For the sake of this chapter, let's call this conversation/gathering of minds a Student Support Summit, because *yay for alliteration*! At the SSS meeting, we come together with the students' historical data—and yes, you're right—way to go!—this certainly includes historical linguistic data (both from an annual assessment and also from our formative/summative linguistic captures throughout the year).

We should begin each of these with our celebrations of the child. These celebrations should feature holistic celebrations across a variety of lenses, including social-emotional well-being, a list of their interests/passions that we know about, skills and talents they possess (highlighting their linguistic assets), their language journeys, their social journeys, their attendance journeys, etc. Too often we come together around the table and someone asks us to "start with strengths" and teachers will rattle off very surface-level contributions like "They're so nice to their friends." We can move beyond that, can't we? We can push each other for more specific strengths that are related to multiple lenses of our students.

Then, we can create space to share our specific concerns. We review our students' achievement data and growth data—both for content AND for language, always (even if one is "not a current concern," this should still be a practice). We review the student's samples of speaking, writing, reading, listening, viewing, and representing across content areas. We ask the students' grownups for any thoughts, ideas, concerns, or feedback with us. Then, inevitably, someone at the table (I usually hear this from our school psychologists) will ask the team about a "like peer."

## A "Like Peer"

Guess what? You might not believe it, but I'm itchy again. So here's the thing, friends. Maybe you've seen this, too. Someone at the table of the Student Support Summit suggests that we compare the current main character with a secondary character (another student). "Is this similar to what their 'like peers' are doing?"

"Oh, let me select another kid to compare them to real quick."

At this point, another person at the table will pull out another random multilingual learner and say "GOT ONE!" just because both students have been identified by the state as a multilingual learner. Just like that. That quickly. Umm, what? How were you able to identify a "like peer" that quickly? Were you going through all of the different pieces that impact language growth and development for two students you serve? Were you reviewing their full linguistic journey and literacy journeys mentally in your mind in a matter of seconds? Or . . . did you just grab another student who's in the same class who shares the same language. "Frankie speaks Ukrainian and he's an eight-year-old third grader, and so is Johnny! So they're 'like peers!'" Umm. No, it's really not that simple.

The practice of identifying a "like peer" might not be truly helpful at all because it's really hard to find one. It's comparing apples to oranges, as they say. Every student is SO different. The umbrella of multilingual learners boasts a VERY LARGE and

VERY DIVERSE group. Just because two students have the same language background doesn't mean that they're a "like peer." Their unique linguistic journeys are important!

## Engaging Families Throughout These Processes

We will examine oppressive family engagement practices in Chapter 7, but one piece that must be mentioned here is that we shouldn't be ignoring the families and grownups of students at any step (in any process). Actively engaging in multiple conversations about goals, growth, concerns, and celebrations should be a part of the process. Yes, of course—language access matters here!

> ### Voices from the Field
>
> #### Dr. Denise Furlong, Author of Voices of Newcomers
>
> In meetings in which decisions are made regarding programming or placement of learners, families must be welcomed and considered to be integral parts of their child's educational journey. If a learner is being evaluated for special education services, the IEP process and all documentation must be available in the home language. Access to this information with explanations for what these decisions may mean for their child are critical for families to truly understand as they make potentially life-altering decisions for their child. As a parent, I found the amount of information in these documents to be overwhelming—even though I am an educator and a native speaker of the language. Ensuring that these documents, these meetings, and these processes are fully understood by families is of paramount importance.

# Let's Go!

Throughout the tiered structures and systems within our schools, we must consistently apply a language lens so that we are upholding our commitments to equity for multilingual learners. By recognizing the importance of the entire system being EL-conscious, we can ensure that our protocols, practices, and assessments are appropriate. We can continue to uplift and elevate our work while committing to collaboratively Question, Equip, and Act throughout our tiered programming.

Let's go! Let's Ignite Real Change!

**TABLE 5.2** Question, Equip, Act (Chapter 5)

| Question | Equip | Act |
|---|---|---|
| How many times are our multilingual students assessed in our system? Why? Is this more than other students? | Consider who are the providers of tiered services in your system for reading and literacy. | Grab your school's MTSS protocol (if you don't have a written policy, jot down notes about your current process). Highlight all the parts that indicate a specific reference to multilingual learners. Analyze the moments where equity for multilingual learners may be at risk in your process. |
| Besides taking tests, what other methods do we use to gather evidence of learning? | Gather information about the tiered intervention programs used in your school and inquire with the developers of those programs about what student groups were used in their norming process. | |
| Do the teachers in my system have EL certification? Are they EL-conscious? How do I know? Whose job do they think it is to support the language of different content areas? | Collect information about how many multilingual learners are receiving tier 2 and tier 3 interventions in reading and math. Is it proportionate to your whole student population? | Specify where/when in your MTSS process families are initially contacted and when they are provided with updates. Analyze how this communication is shared (and in what languages). |

*(Continued)*

**TABLE 5.2** (Continued)

| Question | Equip | Act |
|---|---|---|
| | Explore what types of professional learning opportunities are provided to leaders of MTSS processes and tiered intervention providers that are specific to serving and supporting multilingual learners.<br><br>Grab a few samples of progress monitoring prompts that are used in your system. Scan for any "assumed experiences" that are referenced. | Schedule an annual Multilingual Data Retreat Meeting. Don't have a full multilingual team? Invite the multilingual teacher and a few trusted colleagues to engage in this work together. Everyone deserves a supportive team. |

# 6
# Dismantling Barriers for Advanced, Gifted, Enrichment Access

"Our pacing guides for this class are pretty fast. If he can't keep up, he probably should go back to the grade-level class. This class is advanced for a reason."

This was the emailed response that a colleague of mine shared with me, after the EL teacher and classroom teacher advocated to have a multilingual student placed in their school's advanced math class. The advanced math teacher reported that the student stopped doing the homework and didn't seem interested in participating during class. The EL teacher asked if the teacher was still supporting the languaging needs of this student. When prompted, the teacher emailed that response back.

THROW. THE. FLAGGGG.

Multilingual learners have been historically underrepresented in gifted programs. Students of color have also been historically underrepresented in these programs.

Your school or district might have an equity statement somewhere in their mission, vision, or strategic plan, but this is one piece of the school experience pie that has historically marginalized multilingual learners. Does your gifted program also have an equity statement? Is it evident in the identification process?

## Early Learning Inequities

The inequities that are present in early learning are entirely too large to measure. From early childhood centers, to preschool centers, to daycare centers, there are tons of really glam options available to the wealthiest in our communities. There are beautifully designed daycare centers that cost more than most Americans' mortgages. Some of these centers even boast extra "enrichment opportunities" like art classes, martial arts lessons, and even cooking classes—all for additional fees. These ritzy day care centers prey on the insecurities of the rich and privileged, and so those rosters often fill up and those day care centers make tons of money for their CEOs.

Meanwhile, those with less wealth and privilege have access to much fewer options in their community, and the inequities begin. Now—please hear me very clearly here—if I don't have access to an early learning center, this does not mean my child isn't learning. My child is learning TONS. However, my young child might not be getting daily individualized lessons from a certified early learning educator on early learning literacy and numeracy skills.

In addition to other factors, early childhood centers begin our inequity journeys that position some kids at an advantage and other kids at a disadvantage. There are early learning programs that states will often design that are meant to mitigate these inequities, but the programs are often full and have incredibly long waiting lists. These also still rely on an available adult to be able to transport their child safely each day before and after program hours. That requires the adults' work hours that are conducive to these early learning program hours, a driver's license, access to a vehicle, insurance, and gas money.

> ## Voices from the Field
>
> ### Anonymous Mother of a Multilingual Student
>
> I was born in another country, but three of my four kids were born here in the US. When my daughters went to kindergarten, I was told that they were behind their classmates because they couldn't read yet. I thought, "Isn't that why we're here? Aren't you supposed to teach my kid how to read?" I got frustrated because I felt like the school was judging me. It felt like all the other parents put their kids in these fancy programs when they were little and we just couldn't afford that, so we didn't. But I read to my kids constantly. We baked and cooked together. I told them stories about my childhood. Then I was made to feel ashamed and behind because my kids weren't in preschools or fancy programs for little kids. Why can't we let kids just be kids?

## Community Perceptions

The entire school community might have a different definition of what it means to be gifted. School staff members as well as families and guardians will tend to draw on their own lived experiences (including the good, the bad, and the ugly), as well as the lived experiences of those in their immediate social circles and networks, and bring those experiences into drawing their own definitions and understandings of what giftedness means. This influences how they perceive the "correctness" or "incorrectness" of how their school system views, identifies, and serves gifted learners.

It is important to note that community members might not have a solid understanding of what giftedness is or how it can be represented in different students.

## Staff Perceptions

A lack of linguistic scaffolding is an equity issue. Gifted/Enrichment Educators are still legally required to provide language access to multilingual learners.

Many staff have inherited a problematic and incredibly false belief that a multilingual learner is a "struggling learner" or a "struggling reader." This is absolutely not true. When mindsets have gone unchecked and unchallenged, staff members will lack the proper skills in identifying gifted multilingual learners.

Can a student with interrupted formal education be gifted? YES. Can a student who has gaps in their foundational math and literacy skills be gifted? YES. Are we trained in how to identify giftedness in these student groups? Probably not. Our focus, historically and still today, has been to remediate and provide students with the opportunities to acquire these foundational skills before providing enrichment opportunities, because we're trying to prioritize what we think students need.

Teachers and leaders need ongoing professional learning support that helps them to challenge their assumptions and beliefs about gifted students and what giftedness is and entails. Remember that professional learning might include reviewing student profiles, discussing student scenarios, observing in gifted classrooms, analyzing current matrices and policies, and more.

## Student Perceptions

If I am a student of any age, I likely want to be in spaces where my friends are. If none of my friends are in gifted classes, I may not pursue the chance to be in those classes. Additionally, if no one in the gifted class looks like me or sounds like me, I may not see myself in that space. Furthermore, if students perceive that the teacher of that class is racist—and there's only that one teacher in the gifted program—they may (understandably) have no interest at all. Yes, that sounds like an extreme example. And yes, that was actually expressed to me out loud by a young person of color who was also multilingual.

## Empowering Families and Guardians

If you take a look at your district processes and policies around gifted eligibility and placement, and all of that information is only provided in English, if you listen carefully you can hear a booming, "THROW THE FLAG!" Meaning, the red one. A red flag. If your school or district hosts an information night or webinar to explain the process to families each year, and the information is only presented in English, you'll again hear my father yell from the back, "THROW THE FLAG!"

> ### Voices from the Field
>
> #### Anonymous EL Teacher
>
> I taught 6th grade multilingual students and I supported them across a few content areas. Whenever I was in Frankie's math class, I noticed he would do all the work during the lesson, and then pull out a book to read for the rest of class. He flew through each of the problems. He would grab his device to translate when needed. I talked to his mom and she told me how much he loved math and that was his favorite subject at his old school. We both commented that he already knew all the material and needed to be challenged, so we together wrote a letter to the math teacher, principal, and curriculum director. This led to us having a meeting and the team agreed to place Frankie in accelerated math. He absolutely thrived and seemed much happier.

## Screenings

As part of most school and district processes for identifying gifted students, there is generally a universal screener that is given to all students. If they fall within a certain score range, they might be placed on a list to dig into further for eligibility for a gifted program. We want to ensure that the universal screener is not linguistically or culturally biased. Many districts have moved from using heavily language-based prompts in their assessment instruments to instead using measures with more non-linguistic prompts, in an effort to use a less biased instrument.

One of the biggest hurdles to accessing a gifted program is harsh cutoff scores, meaning if your percentile doesn't fall within a certain range, your eligibility is stopped in its tracks and there is no other pathway to gaining admittance.

## Multi-Step Identification Process

As schools and districts examine how to make their admittance process more equitable, they've unpacked their entrance criteria. I've seen great examples of schools that have moved from rigid flowcharts consisting of harsh cut scores to having multiple entrance ramps that reflect a more linguistically and culturally responsive process.

Some schools and districts have incorporated the use of additional data pieces, including other assessment scores. This might include state assessment data, district-wide benchmark data, or even local assessments used in the classroom.

Additionally, some schools have created opportunities to gather narratives from educators. This provides the opportunity for stakeholders to share additional data pieces, including relevant anecdotal information, classroom-level noticings and examples, and more. Integrating the sharing of narratives can help to expand opportunities for students who would previously remain unidentified.

Furthermore, families have been integrated into this process by also having the opportunity to share narratives about their children with the school system. *This step in itself needs to be a multifaceted system of narrative sharing.* Families must be able to provide this narrative in a linguistically responsive way—meaning that multiple pathways must be created to share information. For example, if families would like to orally share this information in their preferred and/or heritage language, we must ensure we create this opportunity for them to do so. This might mean we have dedicated time and space for a visit with the family (ensure that the family has transportation access to the school) with a high-quality interpreter (more on this in the next chapter). This might mean we encourage families to provide a written narrative in their preferred language—and that we as the school district own the responsibility to have that narrative translated. This might mean that if a family member wants to provide a written narrative to the team but they don't have literacy skills, that we provide a time and space for them to sit with someone who can write what is dictated.

## Transparent Process

The school and district should be transparent about the process for identifying gifted students. *Transparency builds trust.* If the school or district is not transparent about something (anything), this allows for community members to fill in the blanks with their best guesses and their worst assumptions, and also engage in rumor spreading. Being transparent is good for everyone!

In terms of transparency about this specific process, we have to examine how accessible our transparency efforts are. Is there a spot on the school website where we share each step of our process? Are there copies of the process and the policies available in EVERY language of the student and family population? Or, do you simply have your "top 5" languages? Or do you have only English information on your website?

When you have information-sharing opportunities, like a webinar or family event during the school day, after school, or in the evening—are all families provided with language access? Do you advertise that you will have language access at each of these offerings? And HOW do you advertise this language access?

## Appeals Process

Sometimes, a district will offer a family/guardian the option to appeal in the case that their student is deemed ineligible after that first initial round of screenings and narrative/data collection. Folks may say that this can be a step to make the process more equitable. Alright—sounds great, unless it's only great for some families.

Sharing this specific part of the process needs to be done very intentionally in order to communicate that this is an open invitation and that this is the right of all families. Did you know that in some cultures it's considered disrespectful to disagree with a titled educator? It is. Some cultures would never disagree with the decision of a teacher or a principal because they believe it's insulting and shows distrust. The appeals process itself assumes an individualist rather than collective worldview. The US is a highly individualist society. Other countries are at different places and spaces in the collective/individualist archetype. The process itself might be new to me, especially if my culture and my home country don't have this type of process. This might mean that you'd likely have more American-born families/guardians going through with this part of the process.

Of those American-born families/guardians, this part of the process (the appeal) may be reserved to families with certain privileges. For example, if I were to receive this notice about the opportunity to appeal, I would need to reserve time in my schedule to work on my portion of the appeal process. If I had to write a statement, this assumes I have literacy skills to do this, or I have access to someone who can support me in this. I might need to research and view a few samples of a formal written appeal, just so I know what it should include. I'm not sure how easy it will be to locate samples in my language, especially if my home country doesn't have this process.

If I don't have literacy skills to navigate this part of the process, am I completely out of luck, or is there a different avenue I can take? I may worry that if I admit I don't have literacy skills, the school will assume my family is unintelligent and/or poorly educated, and that will count against my child in this process. Can

I just call someone I trust at the school to tell them my thoughts on the phone? Do I have someone I trust at the school to begin with to have this conversation? Do they speak my language?

Being able to correctly submit the appeal would also be important. Do I have to submit this electronically? Are the directions clear? Does the school district assume that I have a Gmail account in order to submit via a Google Form? Is the form available in my language? Does the school clearly tell me that I can write this appeal in my own language?

### Voices from the Field

#### Anonymous EL Teacher

> My 8th grade student was gifted, and I knew it. He always thought outside the box and came up with creative solutions. He absolutely stood out from his peers in terms of his ability. Our school district had just revamped our eligibility systems for placing students into the gifted program. There was an Appeals Process where families could write a letter to advocate for their child if the first round of data collection didn't show that their child got a certain score. I called the mom and talked to her. I shared that every parent has the right to appeal. At first she seemed unsure, but after we talked, we decided to write the appeal letter together. After we wrote the appeal and sent it off, she shared that she initially didn't want to appeal because she thought the school would find her argumentative. I assured her this was not the case, but I understood where she was coming from.

I've also heard stories of powerful privileged parents in a community banding together and threatening to sue the school district if their children don't make it into the program.

You can see that this appeals process sounds really great in theory, but the actual methods are really important here. Language access and explicit mentioning of language access at every step of the way is critical if we want this to be linguistically accessible to all families. If we're not doing this, we're just offering linguistically privileged families/guardians the chance to appeal.

When the appeals are complete, determining who is around the table discussing each appeal is also a really important piece of this conversation. It is my hope that these folks would remain steadfast to an equitable process for all students.

## Provisional Acceptance

Sometimes a district or school will grant "provisional access" to gifted programming as a trial for a unit or two to see if the student can hack it. After those weeks, if the students' scores or performance don't match that of the expectation, they may be dropped from the program.

This provisional acceptance can feel a whole lot like a compromise to appease parents with privilege who complain about how the entrance of these "other" students will impact their child. Using a provisional acceptance will appease whoever is advocating for the multilingual learners, to whom they can return and say, "Well, we gave it a try for Frankie, but it looks like they couldn't handle the rigor of the class. At least we gave it a shot!"

## Gifted Class Caps

While staffing challenges are an issue, and our school only has one gifted educator, it is customary to limit the class size to the top percentiles. Those class caps can also be barriers to students who don't "make it" under the school or district's traditional methods.

If there are 42 students who are deemed eligible, then it's the school district's responsibility to meet their needs. Figure it out.

## Shaking Up Our Systems

It is important to note the correlation between power and privilege and how that comes into play in many communities' understandings of gifted programming. Many of those families/guardians and other folks with power and privilege will feel that this process has allowed Pandora's Box to be opened and be afraid or angered (or both) that this may jeopardize their own child's access to the gifted program.

Here are some quotes given by community members (in this case they identified themselves as "concerned parents") from a few unnamed school district board of education meeting minutes when districts have tried to make their gifted programming more equitable.

> "I don't need all that equity crap invading the gifted program. We have to have some limits."
>
> "So are we just letting anyone in now? Is that the goal? I don't want our district's gifted program to just be a free-for-all. It has to mean something."
>
> "If we water down the learning of the gifted program, what will that mean for my kid? Their learning is going to be impacted. That's not fair to my kid."
>
> "My kid shouldn't have to suffer because of these equity committees."
>
> "These spots should be reserved for kids whose families have invested in education. My own family has always invested in private tutors to ensure that my child performs at the top, and their achievement shouldn't be minimized just to give a less fortunate kid an opportunity. Maybe their parents should be more involved."

Wow. That last one boils my blood every time I see it. But yeah, it's a reality. And this is just the folks who felt confident and empowered enough to go up to the mic and submit their comments at a board meeting. Imagine what else they're thinking that they didn't say publicly?

If your district has done any work in this area, or perhaps if you've heard of a neighboring district engaging in this work, I'd encourage you to explore your public board of education's meeting minutes. Do you see comments like this? Perhaps you've heard these comments outside of board meetings. What are folks saying?

District leaders need to be prepared to have these real conversations and help build a greater sense of understanding amongst the community. There are many privileged and powerful families who are fearful that the presence of "others" in "their" programs will be catastrophic or otherwise harmful to their own privileged child. It's on district leaders to remain steadfast to their commitments to equity, especially in the face of power and privilege with really loud, public voices.

## Detracked Honors and Earned Honors

There are some school districts in Illinois that have begun to detrack their honors programming. They've gotten creative with how to create more equitable opportunities for historically marginalized students to participate meaningfully in honors programs.

Instead of offering a separate "honors level" class, all students in every class are given the opportunity to submit extra work in order to earn the honors credit requirement. The rigor remains high, the expectation remains high, and every student has the opportunity to go for it if they'd like. Doing this has opened doors for multilingual learners who may have otherwise been denied the opportunity.

## Being "Accepted" into the Program

Yeah, I used quotation marks there purposefully, because being "accepted"—as in, you're "allowed in"—is one thing; it's another to be "accepted" by the teacher and by the classmates and experience a sense of belonging.

So let's imagine that a few multilingual learners have now gained admittance (for real) to the gifted program. What safeguards are in place to ensure that the instruction is linguistically supportive and accessible to all students? What professional learning and/or coaching is being provided to the educators of that program? Remember, free and appropriate public education is a civil right for all students. Appropriate means accessible.

I know how hard it is to find teachers who have multiple certifications. We often call these types of teachers "unicorns." For example, if a teacher has both an EL endorsement along with a special education endorsement, we'd call them a "unicorn" because they'd have both areas of specialization and could teach across multiple roles and contexts. The same is true for teachers who have Gifted endorsements and also an EL endorsement. Because I know how difficult this is to find in one human being, I would recommend that the gifted course with multilingual learners be co-taught with an EL-endorsed (*and* EL-conscious) educator.

Having the gifted class co-taught would elevate the instructional practices and behaviors of the gifted teacher and also the multilingual learner teacher. This would also create a higher probability that the instruction is being delivered through the language lens.

I would advocate in this case for the co-taught model rather than merely a collaborative teaching model. In a collaborative teaching model, it could include anything from collaborative planning through unit design or lesson design, or it could include in-class support. Remember that in-class support is not the same as co-teaching. Co-teaching is the full and complex process of co-planning, co-instructing across multiple models, co-assessing, and co-reflecting (that requires full systems-level support from administration, including dedicated time for co-planning). This four-step process shared between two professionals would best meet the unique needs of gifted multilingual learners.

## Monitoring the Experience

If students in the gifted class are experiencing peer-to-peer microaggressions on the daily, how well do you think the student would perform? If the student is attending classes where their peers often make statements about how immigrants "should go back to where they came from," how well will this student want to do? If I was a child and I was faced with this treatment, this rhetoric, and this learning environment, I would do anything to get out. It feels unsafe.

Likewise, if I am a student and I have the fear that *the teacher* has demonstrated any of these behaviors, I will also recognize that the teacher is unsafe. I would do anything to get out.

It's not enough to "get kids into the program" if they're subjected to emotional or psychological harm during class every day. What structures are in place for students to share their honest experiences throughout the course? Remember, it's not always safe for ALL students to share, even if the teacher "declares" that it is a safe space, or if they pop up a poster on the wall. There may be some students in the class who feel super safe sharing their thoughts and opinions, and others know that their voice isn't as safe.

 ## Let's Go!

It is important that we examine how accessible our gifted and advanced programs are for multilingual learners. We must identify our criteria, assessment measures, and processes for gaining access to these programs. Additionally, we must continue to reflect and monitor how linguistically accessible these courses are for multilingual learners. Finally, it is important that we continue to check our system to see how equitable the experience is for multilingual learners within advanced and gifted programs. We can continue to Question, Equip, and Act so that multilingual learners have every opportunity to thrive in every program!

Let's go! Let's Ignite Real Change!

**TABLE 6.1** Question, Equip, Act (Chapter 6)

| Question | Equip | Act |
|---|---|---|
| What is your school's process for gaining entrance into advanced, AP, gifted/enrichment, or Honors courses? 

How transparent is our school's process? Why is this? As a community member, where can I find this information? Why is it housed there?

Do all families have opportunities to learn about the identification process? How do you know that all families have this information? | Look at the student rosters in your advanced, AP, gifted/enrichment, or Honors courses. Is there an over- or underrepresentation of multilingual students in these courses?

Collect information about how all staff have been given professional learning about identifying giftedness in all students AND identifying giftedness in multilingual students.

Collect information about unit design and instructional practices that are linguistically supportive of multilingual students.

Gather student, family, and staff perception data of who "belongs" in advanced, AP, gifted/enrichment, or Honors courses. | Ensure that your school's process is transparent and available in multiple languages to all members of the community.

Review your identification criteria to ensure that students at all proficiency levels have opportunities to participate.

Expect that all advanced, AP, gifted/enrichment, or Honors courses have linguistic scaffolds embedded and identified into unit and lesson design.

Create and meet with focus groups of multilingual students who are in advanced, AP, gifted/enrichment, or Honors courses. Listen to and believe their lived experiences. |

# 7

# Dismantling Oppressive Family Engagement Practices and Designing Equitable Supports

I walked in from the rain, ready to volunteer at a school building in my district to interpret for parent-teacher conferences, as no one in this particular building spoke Spanish. I met up with the waiting teacher outside of her classroom. She excitedly greeted me and thanked me for being there.

> "Oh gosh—this is so fantastic to have someone here to interpret for conferences! We've literally never had this before!" I could faintly hear my father in the background of my mind "THROW THE FLAG!" but I tried to quiet the voice down enough to ask her, "What did you do in the past when you needed an interpreter?"
>
> I hope you're sitting down for this, friend.
>
> "Oh, I would just ask the kids to interpret. They could usually do it just fine."
>
> *RED FLAGS STREAM DOWN AND MAKE A LARGE RED FLAG MOUNTAIN.*
>
> I tried to gather my thoughts enough to confirm, "You asked the students to interpret their own conferences?"
>
> "Yes!" she replied excitedly. "Thank goodness they're bilingual, right?"

DOI: 10.4324/9781003514381-7

So sorry, reader. I couldn't find you for a second. We were buried in red flags. Before you ask—yes, this was reported. Because YES—this is illegal. Like, super-duper illegal.

"But, Carly—this is an award-winning school." Mmkay. I'm sure it does great things for kids and families of privilege. What awards did it win?? Do those awards mention the illegal practices that are happening? Was the award for being in violation of the families' civil rights?

## Declaring That Some Families Are "Not Involved"

We have got to stop name-calling. We don't allow students to do it, then when the kids are gone for the day, we do it. Does calling families you serve "uninvolved" or "disengaged" bring you a sense of satisfaction? I'm genuinely curious. If you call a family "uninvolved," does that absolve you of your work with them? Does it dictate how you will treat them? Does it excuse the way you dismiss them?

Let's do some further uprooting here. Let's really put our backs into this time. SCRAAAPE that carpet, friend. There's a lot baked into the fibers here.

We (all of us, myself included) do not have the authority to judge a family, a parent, a guardian, or grownup of any of our students. We don't know them deeply, understand their lived experiences or understand their full current realities, and we've never walked in their shoes. Perhaps you've experienced some similar hardships or stories that they've maybe shared with you, or perhaps one part of your identity is the same or similar to those—those isolated shared stories can give you a false sense of "knowing what ___ is like," but you still don't know their shoes and the entirety of their stories and lived experiences.

We tend to make massive assumptions about families/ grownups of the students we serve based on whether or not they attend an isolated event—like a "parent-teacher conference." This is problematic for many reasons.

As a human being with white privilege, middle class privilege, and language privilege, I can recognize within myself that if I go to a school-related event once and it doesn't feel good, or I have one person there that rubs me the wrong way, I'm far less likely to attend that event in the future. Even if there's a cute sign on the door that tells me that I'm welcome. If the overall experience wasn't positive, I probably won't be interested in going back. If the overall experience included microaggressions (by either staff or other grownups), dirty looks, or exclusionary moments (like not having language access to either social conversations or the content of the event), you can bet I will never want to come back, even if it's a year later and my child has a different teacher. That one experience taught me that I was not welcome.

If the experience of whatever event isn't positive, how are we to name-call the family and deem them "uninvolved?" Well, for one—it's MUCH easier for folks in the school to say this rather than take any type of ownership or responsibility for how the event felt. Furthermore, we often don't offer community debriefs after larger (or even smaller) events, like the Math Night or the Parent-Teacher Conference. We never actively collect feedback from the grownups, so it's much more convenient to blame them, shrug our shoulders, and move on.

This is why our family/grownup community needs to have opportunities to share their experiences—but the HOW of this is really important. Is it done through an in-person meeting? Is it a survey? Is it an anonymous feedback form?

If you opt for in-person debriefs in small groups, let's look at a few layers that we must consider (aside from transportation, childcare, and language access). First, we have to ask who is leading these debriefs. It must be someone who is familiar and can establish a sense of trust (likely over time). If I ask members of our family/grownup community to come in and debrief an event with me, how do I cultivate a sense of trust with them so that we all feel comfortable enough to share? Remember, we can't just call something a "safe space" in order to make it a safe space. Next, we need to BELIEVE people when they share something that may be tough to hear. It was likely very difficult for them to share it in the first place, so if we dismiss their experience altogether because it reflects badly on our system, then these feedback sessions are just for optics.

## Language Access

What's legal and what's not? We must provide language access to families for both written and verbal communication. If you don't have a multilingual staff, you should look at what you're doing to attract and retain multilingual staff members. Districts need to be responsible for building up their interpreter and translator resources. How are we engaging our community? How are we partnering with local organizations? How are we supporting the training that goes into being a highly qualified interpreter? How are we leveraging additional resources, like contracting with outside language vendors (either through a phone service, Zoom service, or other)?

It is not sufficient for us to utilize Google Translate when families come in for conferences. It is illegal (and also downright ridiculous) to ask children, no matter their age, to interpret for their families for conferences.

## PTA

Full transparency—I've never been a PTA Mom. I've seen lots of movies and TV shows that depict the PTA as a snobby, cliquey group of very connected and very privileged grownups in a school community. I cannot imagine that they're all that way. This is a great time for folks like me to check my bias, and this is a great time for all of us to challenge that narrative!

How linguistically inclusive is your PTA or PTO? Does the PTA meeting offer hybrid events where folks without transportation can still be involved? Do the meetings have language access? I already know that the invitations are not just in English only (because wouldn't that just be silly?). Will certain grownups be shunned if they bring their younger children to the meetings? How accessible is it to run for an elected PTA position? Does the election process privilege some grownups over others?

Sometimes school leadership is afraid to step on the toes of the families/grownups who are participating in the PTA of their own free will, and we don't want to "bite the hand that feeds us," especially since the PTA consists of volunteers from the school community and they're not getting paid for this. They often raise funds for fun things we do at school. Most times they're in charge of "appreciating the teachers" (that's another book entirely, friends), so we really don't want to be "rude" to this group and suggest that they're not really being that inclusive to the entire school community.

So . . . you're right. Because they're "so nice" we shouldn't expect them to, at the very least, be linguistically inclusive. Umm. That sounds weird when we say it like that, right?

The school or district leader might gather all of the PTA leaders and offer ongoing workshops about language access, bias, cultural competencies, communication practices, and much more! This would be a great way to elevate the entire system and create more opportunities for systematic changes.

## Board Meetings

Does your entire family community understand the purpose of your district's Board of Education? Do they know that the board members are locally elected officials, and that they do monthly in-person meetings to make decisions about what goes on in schools? Some boards do a monthly feature of different teachers or classrooms, or even have students share routinely about what they're learning about or experiencing in their classroom. "All community members are welcome" to attend the "open portion" of the board meeting, at least that's usually a statement on the board's page of the district website. If your board meeting doesn't have language access for families, it's exclusionary and only provides information to those with language privilege.

## Family Liaison Roles

Some schools and districts have utilized or have begun utilizing a Family Liaison role. These roles are absolutely incredible opportunities to make meaningful connections between the school and families we serve. Finding the right person for this role is critical. In collectivist cultures, the community is close and relies on each other for important information. This also includes perception and experiences. For example, if I had a really great experience with a teacher, you can bet I've probably shared that with my network. On the flip side, if I had a really negative or problematic experience with a teacher, or at a school event, I will likely have shared that with my network as well. Some will call this a gossip circle—some may call this a community sharing our lived experiences. If the community feels that the liaison is reliable and trustworthy, the circle will embrace this person.

I've seen this role *mostly* utilized for serving linguistically diverse communities. When this is the case, this role needs specific professional learning in cultural competencies. Any role that is family or community-facing must be given professional learning support in connecting with families from around the world. Sometimes a human resources department will say something like, "This person is a great fit because they speak Spanish/Ukrainian/Russian/Haitian Creole!" Cool! I love to hear about the language gifts that folks possess. But remember, just because they can speak the same language doesn't mean they're going to automatically know how to connect meaningfully. Plus, languages are broad and can span over multiple countries or parts of the world. They also span over multiple layers of identity, culture, and deep culture.

Clear expectations need to be provided to staff about when to engage the liaison, when to loop them in, and when to use your own resources. When this is not clearly communicated, there will be teachers that will make the assumption that if it is the family of a multilingual student, all communication should get funneled through the family liaison role. This is not the case. We have to be very careful and thoughtful about how we utilize this role, because strong family communication is everyone's responsibility.

If districts create and fill this position in their systems, they will often say "this person serves as an advocate for families."

This sounds lovely. But if this position is created to offer the district or the community an "equity solution," we should pause. Let's together wonder why we need one role to advocate on behalf of an entire family population. Let's wonder what we're doing with the positions we already have and *why they're not advocating*. Is it that we don't have familiarity with laws? That's not good. Is it that we ourselves have underdeveloped cultural competency skills? It feels like we should invest in that. Is it that our current staff doesn't feel like they have advocacy power or skills? I think we should all build those skills up and empower every adult in this area. Is it because other positions don't have time for dedicated family engagement? Let's consider what this position needs to advocate for (or against) at school. If this position is meant to mitigate our inequitable school system, then this isn't real, true Equity. If we don't address this, then this one person will become the funnel of support and "advocacy."

When this happens, and one role is turned into (either intentionally or unintentionally) MULTILINGUAL FAMILY ADVOCATE, how do we support this role? When they bring forward the concerns of the community, how do we, as a full system (collectively and individually) act on those concerns? How do we support the system in moving towards proactivity vs. reactivity? How do we maintain a sense of trust for the liaison role? My worry is always that this one person will become burnt out after not being supported by the district players in their work.

I think this role is an important one, but I think this role needs a lot of attention and care that districts don't realize ahead of creating the position. If your system is not going to act on the systematic concerns that are being brought forward by the families themselves or by the district-appointed advocate/liaison, then having the position feels performative (and also, do some major uprooting here about why).

## Communication Preferences

I have some friends who are texters, some who prefer direct phone calls, and some who do everything through email only.

I have some folks in my life who are super active on social media and others who have either closed all of their accounts or never had them to begin with. Every human being has their own preferences about how they best like to give and receive communication. The grownups of our students are no different! We have to have a robust system with multiple platforms to hit all different types of communicators in our systems. And—do I sound like a broken record yet?—we must look at which of those platforms provide language access to families.

## Accessible Websites and Platforms

If you have a tiny widget on your school or district website that allows families to click to change the language—but no one knows about it and it's difficult to see upon first opening up the website—it's not a linguistically accessible website. Additionally, if the widget doesn't appear at all on a cellular device, it's not an accessible website.

How your website is designed at either the school or district level is really important, because it can serve as a portal to necessary information.

Online staff directories can be especially tricky. I would recommend enabling a few different filters in your sorting mechanism so that I can group teachers in different ways (grade levels, content areas, club sponsors, etc.). I may not always know the name of my child's teachers (again, don't assume that I'm uninvolved here—maybe assume that your communication at the school level is not doing what it needs to do). I prefer when there's a picture next to a name, but I can also understand privacy concerns from a safety perspective. However, if there's a portal that only grownups of students can enter, this can go a long way—especially because even if I do know the name of the teacher I'm trying to connect with, I may not know how to spell it.

Please also pay attention to what the teachers are sharing with family members/grownups of their students. Perhaps the verbal "Please don't call me because my classroom phone hasn't worked in three years—email me instead" messages at Curriculum Night directly go against what is offered on the district directory on the webpage (here's the phone number of the staff member).

## Friendly Reminders That Aren't Actually Reminders

This one is going to sound really specific, but stay with me. If your school or district tends to use the term "reminder" incorrectly, it can cause damage. Here's what I mean. If the school text message system sends out a message that says, "Friendly Reminder! Parent-Teacher Conferences are next week! Here's the link to sign up!" If this is the first time I'm hearing about this, it's not a REMINDER—it's BREAKING NEWS. If you call something a reminder and it's not, you have GOT. TO. STOP.

Sometimes people will use this phrase as a greeting. It's not a greeting. It's a note about what type of communication this is, and mislabeling it is a problem.

If I receive a message that has the term "friendly reminder" it insinuates that you (the school or district) have already given me this information before. If I receive this and feel caught off guard, it can do a few things. First, it may give me (the parent/family/guardian/grownup) a sense of shame that I forgot this thing. "Oh no, I'm so behind! How did I miss this?" Second, it may give me a sense of feeling disconnected from the school—"Did everyone else know about this? How am I the last to know about this?" Third, if I go digging into my email or scrolling the social media account of the school and I see NO communication about this event, it can make me distrust the school. Legit. It feels like a weird gaslight game to suggest that I should've known about this even though they never told me about it.

Oh, also on this note—handing me a calendar at an event in August with the dates of all the stuff throughout the school year is not you notifying me about the parent-teacher conferences that are happening in February. Nope.

Additionally, your school and district public relations team (or person) needs to explore ways to meaningfully connect with families that don't look like them and don't speak the same language as them. This must be non-negotiable. If my job is to tell the story of the school or district, and to communicate effectively with all stakeholders—then I CANNOT PICK AND CHOOSE WHICH STAKEHOLDERS. I must have a plan for my ongoing professional learning in this area, and I must have a plan for how I will continue to connect meaningfully with multilingual families in the school community. I also must be held accountable in this work as a part of my evaluation process from the superintendent.

## Social Media

I love, love, love social media as a means of communication, but I also recognize that not everyone does, as each person has their communication preferences and styles. I would like to share, though, why I love social media so much for family engagement.

For one, I'm on social media anyway, for both personal and professional use. I have an Instagram, a TikTok account, LinkedIn, and I still have my Twitter account (some call it X now). So hey, if my kids' school is on there, that's a great way for me to follow along with upcoming events and happenings at the schools. I *don't* already have a Remind App, a Seesaw App, a Canvas app, etc. I appreciate that I don't have to download an additional app to stay connected with what's happening.

> ### Voices from the Field
>
> #### Anonymous Uncle of Multilingual Learner
>
> My nephew and I were really close when he lived with me in Mexico City, and when he moved I really missed him. The teacher set up an Instagram account where I was given access to view and follow

> because I told my sister to let the teacher know. She would post pictures of what the kids were doing in class and once I got to send my nephew a message to tell him how proud I was of him because he got an award for his math test. Even though I was so far away I could still have the blessing of being connected to him.

Second, one of the things I appreciate most about social media is that the genre of a social media post is usually very concise and digestible, and posts usually include some type of graphic, visual, or video to accompany the post. This means that it is a more linguistically accessible genre rather than an emailed newsletter with loads of paragraphs.

Third, it helps me stay better connected with the learning that's happening. As a family member or the grownup of a student, when I follow my kids' school accounts, this provides a window for me into the learning of classrooms. As my own kids have grown up, our own dinner-table-conversations have morphed over the years. I used to be able to ask my kids when they were younger, "What did you do at school today?" and that would unlock a whole collection of stories, conversations, and experiences. As the years have gone by, and my kids have grown older, if I were to ask them the very same question, they would very naturally shrug and say, "Nothing," or "I don't know." I always laugh at the viral social media posts that show something like Figure 7.1.

When I see this, I laugh out loud because even though most kindergarten students will gleefully fill in their grownups with all the day's happenings, there are some details (even big ones!) that slip their minds when asked hours later! With older kids, they may *not* want to engage with their grownups about all the day's happenings. So if the teacher or school posts a picture of something they did in class, I can hold up that picture and ask my kids a more specific question, "What is happening here?"

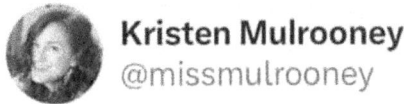

**Kristen Mulrooney**
@missmulrooney

Yesterday I asked my kindergartener what she did in school and she said "nothing," then later I went on Instagram and her teacher had posted a picture of her holding a crocodile.

**FIGURE 7.1** Tweet from Kirsten Mulrooney that shows the power of social media for family engagement.

It unlocks a whole conversation that I may not have had access to otherwise.

Additionally, I can learn about the vibe of the school really quickly based on what's posted on the social media channels. If there are fun videos of the teachers dancing during an assembly, or the school mascot posts a video tiptoeing through the stacks of the library, or there's a bird's eye view video of all the third graders having an impromptu dance party at lunch in the cafeteria, I can gain a sense of the school culture and climate. If it looks fun, I will perceive it as a fun place. The storytelling behind those social media posts can build bridges and cultivate a sense of trust between school and the community.

## The Jump Off a Cliff: Middle School Communication

Something I don't think we talk about enough is the jump in communication efforts between elementary and middle schools. Now, please hear me—I'm not saying middle schools are bad at communication. What I am saying is that the expectations and structures of each school are different. This can (and does) impact grownup perception.

In an elementary school, most teachers are accustomed to designing some type of weekly (or at least monthly) newsletter that shares different happenings and updates. My own child's work is something I can view easily on different platforms like Seesaw or Schoology (assuming the school has taught me a few times how to sign up, navigate it, and use it with regularity). When I have a question about the bus, or I need to share a concern about the school cafeteria, I will often funnel all those questions through the classroom teacher. Even if I know that is not their direct responsibility, that teacher will often connect me with the adult who has the answer. We could explore here how this as a practice impacts an elementary classroom teacher's communication load and overall workload, and how very different that is from other levels.

However, when my child moves into the middle school grades and doesn't just have one teacher, things change. Communication changes drastically. From one teacher having 32 students for almost the entire day and learning most content through that one adult, to now having eight different adults who teach eight different things, it can feel a little like jumping off a cliff. In the past, if I (as the grownup of a child in school) had a question or a concern, I'd often rely on an email or phone call to the classroom teacher.

But now, I have eight different adults to communicate with about eight different school subjects, but who do I call if I have a bus question, or a concern about the school cafeteria, or a question about the PTA? As the grownup of my middle schooler, I may feel at a loss about who to contact.

Additionally, I'm not sure what the expectation is as far as content teachers' creating some sort of a weekly newsletter. Most that I've spoken with and worked with over the years do not do this—and not because they're bad teachers or because they don't value family connections. The structure of their day looks different. They may teach three different preps—so are they expected to create three different newsletters? Umm, that's A LOT. Also, I use the "newsletter" as an example that many teachers are familiar with, and NOT because I think that a newsletter is the best way to communicate with all families. Many times, I don't think it is.

## Weekly Newsletters vs. Ongoing Shorter Boops

I use the noun "boop" to describe a lot of different things. If you own a dog, you might be familiar with the term "nose boop," which basically just means a little loving tap on the nose of your dog. It's quick, it's affectionate, and it appreciates the cuteness of a little dog snoot (another doggy term, in this case, to mean the *nose*).

I will sometimes refer to a quick consideration or idea as a "thought boop" because it's like a nose boop, but for your brain. Communication can also come in small boops.

A boop is nice because it's concise. A social media post, a GIF, a text message, a sentence, or a few phrases can all be quick little boops to communicate something. An ongoing diet of steady boops is great to continue building and cultivating connections. They also demonstrate a notable shift in how we all communicate differently since the onset of the internet (and particularly social media).

A newsletter is much more than a boop. It's a more involved process. Generating newsletters can be time-consuming, and it can also be intimidating to some teachers who don't particularly enjoy writing (I know, I know—*gasp! Not all teachers like writing*. We can unclutch our pearls now). I know plenty of teachers who utilize the assistance of artificial intelligence in order to get something initially generated so they can edit/tweak it before sending it out. Sometimes teachers spend so much time generating these newsletters and it may not have the reward we're hoping it will have.

> ### Voices from the Field
>
> #### Anonymous 5th Grade Classroom Teacher
>
> I hate writing newsletters because they take so long to write. I even started using AI to help me get these done faster but it still took time. After talking with

> my instructional coach about the purpose of a newsletter, we decided to change up the structure a little. At parent-teacher conferences, I asked how my parents wanted to get their information. I had a few samples ready on the table and asked which they thought they'd be able to interact with more as a busy parent. Eventually, I did away with newsletters and I would write shorter sentences through our text message system because that's what my parents used the most. This was awesome because it saved me a lot of time and I actually got so much more engagement and interaction with families by doing this. They told me at the end of the year that they were hopeful that their teachers next year would use this system.

Grownups of kids are busy, and they don't always read the newsletters. Additionally, not all grownups have literacy skills. Also, if it's an e-newsletter, I may not have consistent Wi-Fi access or I don't use my email that much in life, so I don't receive all of them to begin with. As an adult with language privilege and technology/internet privilege, I don't always read them all either. It's not because I'm a bad mother. It's not because I don't value school, education, or my child's teachers. It's because life is real.

So perhaps we can incorporate more frequent, much shorter boops throughout the week/month that might prove to generate more connection opportunities with those we serve.

## Language Access for Events at School

Here again, I'm going to mention language access, but let's talk a little bit more about this at a larger-scale event, because this is nuanced. Simply providing interpreters isn't all you need in order to provide language access to families. It goes beyond just checking that box.

I've seen districts try out a few different things, and I can appreciate the effort to mix it up to see what might work. Taking risks can create better opportunities when serving all, and reflecting or debriefing about these experiences WITH families, AND with our educators/staff, can help us become stronger practitioners.

I've seen districts hire an interpreter to come up and stand alongside whoever the speaker might be at the front. If the English speaker is going through an English slide deck, and the interpreter doesn't also have the slide deck available in the other language, the presentation isn't equally accessible. It still privileges English over the other language.

If the English speaker is going into great details, with small jokes and quick stories and anecdotes, but the interpreter is only providing the audience with the condensed "key points" version of the content, the presentation isn't equally accessible. Sometimes folks are told to do this in the interest of "saving time," but this again points to who is being prioritized in this experience—*saving time for whom?*

I've seen schools do a presentation video with subtitles in other languages, but the content of the video (slides or handouts or other written language) is not translated. So if it's a voiceover of a slide deck, and the slide deck is not translated, then it's not an equally accessible presentation.

I've seen schools and districts provide headphones to families who speak other languages so that they can sit wherever they'd like and have access to a live interpreter (who may be standing in the front of the room, the back of the room, or somewhere else!) from the comfort of their seats.

I've also seen schools and districts FLIP THIS so that the English speakers have to use the headphones while the "main" session is in Spanish or Korean or Ukrainian or another language. It's a really interesting social experiment to watch as English speakers are asked to grab a pair of headphones so that they can access the content! I've seen some eye rolls. I've seen some shrugs and folks put on their headphones, seemingly unbothered. I've also seen straight-up hissy fits from grown folks who feel that their language privilege is in peril: "WHAT?! THIS IS AMERICA! WE SHOULD BE DOING THIS IN ENGLISH! WHY SHOULD I HAVE TO WEAR THESE HEADPHONES?" (My dad and the red flags are also screaming right now, too—but this yelling is directed at the hissy-fit-throwers.)

We don't realize how much we center English in our settings. Some will argue, "Carly, OF COURSE we should center English!" After all, this is the language of instruction. This is the language of the entire staff (in most US cases). Okay, sure. I get it, but let me share an example of how we center English for everything and how other languages are often the afterthought (yes, here comes The After Slap: Family Edition).

Sometimes for certain school events for families, the school looks outward to "bring someone in." The person is 99% of the time an English speaker. They were hired because of their skill, their charisma, their energy, or their talent—whatever. That's fine. That sounds cool. AND ALSO—if the school or district hires this very wonderful and very cool speaker for a family-facing event, and there's an interpreter alongside them, there is likely not the same charisma/energy/passion coming through the interpreter. This is not because the interpreter is bad at their job. No, it's because the interpreter is there to provide the language access, but the DELIVERY of the content will be done quite differently. The interpreter's passion is probably not the same passion as the speaker that was hired. So, when we make decisions about which cool speaker/presenter/expert comes in, how do we prioritize those incredible folks whose preferred or primary language is not English? Perhaps we bring in an incredibly charismatic Mongolian speaker with the energy, passion, talent, and skills and provide the English interpreter. You see?

## School Culture and Climate Starts in the Parking Lot

We've likely all been in a parking lot once or twice before in life where we've observed The Angry Flagger. The Angry Flagger is pissed, but we don't know why. We'll never know if it's because they've been in a three-month state of survival during an incredibly difficult period of their life. We'll never know if they're just in the midst of a bad day. We'll never know if it's because they actually hate children and/or they actually hate their jobs. Who knows! The problem is, when folks don't know, they'll often create their own narratives based on their own evidence or perceptions. That's not good nor is it helpful, but it's what humans do.

The Angry Flagger has an immediate impact on the tone and the vibe of everyone passing through that parking lot—including staff members, families/grownups of kids, and students.

Now, it is not easy or fun to be directing traffic in a school parking lot, especially when you've said the same thing to the same folks FOR MONTHS, and they still are not following directions. Plus, you're outside battling the elements—the sun beating down on you, pouring rain, blizzards, etc. It's not always enjoyable.

The Angry Flagger can set a tone for school culture and climate, and help me as the grownup of a student catch the vibe of the place. If this Angry Flagger is a teacher, I might assume that all the teachers in this building are angry. I may be fearful or uncomfortable if my child is ever in this teacher's classroom. If this Angry Flagger is the principal or assistant principal, I might assume that this person is not approachable about concerns I might have in the future. If the Angry Flagger is a school resource officer, I may have a fear about how safe my child is under their care.

Parking Lot Vibes are important. Remove the Angry Flaggers. Build a cadre of folks who can help build up more positive Parking Lot Vibes. You can go wild and have them randomly dress up as inflatable dinosaurs. You can have them walk around with juice boxes, donut holes, or stickers and walk from car to car to share a friendly greeting. You can carry out a whole karaoke machine and sing songs to the folks waiting in the cars. Does your school have a comfort dog that can (safely) be present in the pickup line. Your school mascot might direct traffic one day. You might have a certain group of students don a very nifty fluorescent safety vest and have the kids become the flaggers (assuming you're doing this very safely, of course). Create a system where if one of your more joyful flaggers is having one of those very-human bad days, you can offer a quick trade out with someone who can muster up some joyfulness.

## School or District Event Planning: Worry About the Vibes

We often spend so much time worrying about the logistics/details of the event and the content of the event, that we overlook a really important piece of the event. Our young people refer to this as The Vibes. The Vibes matter. When I say The Vibes, I am referring to the FEELINGS. Some may call these feelings one piece of the school or district's Culture and Climate.

The Vibes are present in people's facial expressions, tone of voice. The Vibes are in the lighting, the music that might be playing in the space, and in the chatter of the event. The Vibes are present in how folks interact with each other. The Vibes are in the warmth (or coldness) of greetings.

We overlook how important The Vibes are. These are what can make or break an event. From the front door welcome to the closure of the night, we must have more conversations with our teams as we consider what Vibes we're giving to folks as they enter the space.

## Parent-Teacher Conferences

Conferences with interpretation must be prioritized in scheduling. Book these conferences first and then build the rest of the schedule around those. If you leave scheduling the interpreters as the final step, you are creating a hardship for the interpreters' schedules and you may have fewer options.

Additionally, if your district utilizes the same interpreter bank of resources (like, you have one interpreter of that language across the entire district), then you may consider staggering conferences so everyone's not fighting over one human for "conference day."

If you make families come to the parent-teacher conference and it only lasts for ten minutes, you might ask yourself if this poses more hardship for the grownups than it is worth. This is especially true if you're going to just cover (perhaps meaningless) data that paints a picture of their child as "behind" or not doing well, with no plan for support, and no opportunity for parents to share their thoughts or feelings about their own child.

Abandon the "compliment sandwich" and instead be real with parents. Offering three often-unrelated comments can create a sense of distrust and overall misunderstanding of how my child is doing. "So . . . are they doing well?" The compliment sandwich method is inauthentic.

## Don't Bring Your Kids

When there are family or community events at the schoolhouse, and there's a message about not bringing your kids, this is an exclusionary practice. It's also pretty hypocritical messaging: "We love your kids more than anything but don't you dare bring them to the school because this event is only for grownups." If we host an event and the intention is for it to be only for grownups, we may unintentionally be uninviting folks without access to childcare.

For families to secure trusted childcare, there is a level of privilege involved. First of all, I must be able to pay for this. It requires a sense of connectedness within my community. If I just moved here and I'm just getting settled, I might not have connections yet where I feel safe enough to leave my children with someone I'm just getting to know.

If the school can swing childcare, or at the very least offer activities for kids who arrive with their families, do it. Please do not shame families who don't have options.

## Staff Directory: Who Is Who?

This one is low-hanging fruit. Putting a face to a name is important. If the school provides a quick, easy handout or pamphlet of the staff members that me (or my student) will see most often—with their names/roles and faces—I will feel more comfortable communicating with and attending events at the school, because I can recognize the players. It's also helpful to have 1–2 forms of communication for each staff member listed (some staff may prefer email while others prefer a phone call, so this may be customized for each staff member).

Additionally, this is a great opportunity for families to learn about all the roles represented at the school. I may not have been aware that the school has a nurse, for example. I may not have known that the school has a social worker who could help my family learn about different resources available to us in the community. I may not have known that there's an 8th grade social studies teacher who looks like us . . .

 **Let's Go!**

Family engagement is everyone's job—and *multilingual family engagement* is ALSO everyone's job. It is crucial that everyone sees that we all have a hand in this work. Everyone must be given annual refresher courses about laws (particularly around language access) and what bare-minimum compliance means. Everyone must be held accountable for moving beyond just basic compliance to being a reflective practitioner who seeks out continued growth opportunities of cultural competencies, family engagement practices, and dismantling problematic or downright oppressive practices. This is not just the role of the principal, the front office, the district PR team, or the family liaison. Everyone must recognize how they individually and collectively can shape and influence a system that is not just inclusive to all families, but a system that seeks to understand and disrupt barriers that we have either created, cultivated, inherited, or sustained that has invited some families in and kept others out. We can collectively elevate our system as we all Question, Equip, and Act to meaningfully engage with the families and grownups of our multilingual learners.

Let's go! Let's Ignite Real Change!

TABLE 7.1 Question, Equip, Act (Chapter 7)

| Question | Equip | Act |
|---|---|---|
| In my school, whose responsibility is it to provide language access to families? | Collect information about your school's digital presence (school website, e-newsletters, and social media accounts). | When planning for events at the school, consider any potential barriers or difficulties this may pose in advance, and whenever possible, make a plan to directly address those. |
| What are the laws for family communication? Where might I find that information? | Gather different samples of communication that goes home to families. Record any noticings and wonderings and share those with your colleagues. | When we mess up, own it. Take accountability. Apologize. |
| How do I tend to communicate with families? How/why did I make that decision? | Explore different tools that provide language access. Find out what other districts use. | Set a weekly or monthly time in your calendar where you reach out to meaningfully connect with families (write an email, make a phone call, etc.). |
| How often do I communicate with all families? How often do I connect with families of multilingual learners? | Connect with folks at other buildings and discuss ways they've communicated with families. Discuss ways they've meaningfully connected with families. | Ensure this communication is delivered in the family's preferred language. |
| How do I connect with families beyond the walls of the school? How do my colleagues? | | |
| Might we have events that don't feel inclusive to all families? What makes me think so? What might we change? | | |

Dismantling Oppressive Family Engagement Practices ◆ 187

# 8

# Upholding Our Commitments to Equity for Multilingual Learners and Families

Welp. We made it. We Advocated for Equity and we won! WE DID IT!!

Okay, just kidding. BUT WOW, did we explore a LOT together! Are you exhausted? Overwhelmed? Samesies. But are you ready to roll up your sleeves and keep going? Me, too.

I want to personally thank you for sticking with me through this journey. Some of this was really uncomfortable. You heard a lot about my itchiness (and maybe you've shared some itches with me).

## What Is Our Plan for Sustainability as a School or District?

Taking stock of celebrations and milestones can do a lot to fuel this work. A whole lot.

Appreciation and acknowledgement can feel good periodically, but a plaque on the wall isn't going to demonstrate to the recipient that the system is taking on ownership and enacting change for students and families. Sometimes an award can feel performative by the school or district, especially if they treat equity work like a secret so they don't upset their community. The folks doing this work deserve appreciation—yes—but that's not why they're doing this work. They want change. They're demanding change. The best appreciation and acknowledgement for change agents is changed behaviors and more equitable student outcomes!

We must identify specific systems that are going to continuously nourish the leaders of these efforts (remember that these leaders may be teachers, assistants, social workers, coordinators, coaches, the PE teacher, the principal—whoever!). If we don't have a sustainability plan, we are putting our people at risk of burnout, disengagement, or other emotional or psychological harm.

Expecting whoever our leaders are in this work to carry this responsibility alone will be a detriment to our students and families. Our systems cannot afford for us to not intentionally care for those who are taking the lead in this work.

## What Is Our Plan for Our Days Where We Want to Quit This Work?

I need to be equipped with an emergency day that I may need to use so that I can catch my breath, process a moment, or make plans for how I need to proceed in a specific situation. I need to allow myself to take that time to breathe.

Take a break.

Take a breath.

Tell others when you need to tap out so that they can tap in. Be honest. Ask for your help.

## What Is Our Plan for Sustaining Ourselves and Our System in This Work?

There are those who may say that we shouldn't celebrate miniscule wins because they don't transform systems. I wholeheartedly disagree with this. I believe that we should celebrate each small win, because the small moments often have the power to create larger-scale (even systems-level) changes. I think we probably also have to get specific about what people might refer to as a "small win."

Small interactions like a text message, phone call, or an email with a quick note expressing appreciation to a colleague for their work, their question, or their courage at a meeting can really go a long way to build and nurture our allyships. Conversations with teammates that include simple questions like, "Is there another way we might try this?" can work wonders as well. I was once at a meeting where a team was planning an event for families, and a colleague asked her team, "What might happen if we tried streaming the speaker so folks who can't attend physically could still participate?" I watched how posing one question to a team led to a powerful dialogue about inclusive practices for all families. I have no doubt that this one question planted an initial seed that will help guide other decisions about inclusive family practices for future events.

Perhaps we started our first-ever schoolwide book club that centers on multilingual learners. That's definitely not a small win. By having every adult engaging in a sustained and systematic shared learning experience and reflecting together, this has the power to reshape entire pedagogies. That's anything but small.

## How Do I Ask Others for Support?

No matter what my role is in the school system, I must have a channel within my system that I can tap and ask for support. This may come in the form of a question in an email to a boss or a colleague. This may be a request to process a situation with someone. This may be a request for someone I might consider to be an ally to just be next to me during an upcoming meeting. Your best allies might be outside your department, too.

If I'm a teacher, this can come in the form of utilizing my union. Our local and regional unions can absolutely be a space and place to help us fight for justice for our students and families.

They may be able to set aside time to meet with us, answer our questions on our personal email accounts, or send us some tools to use for upcoming interactions.

No matter who I am in the school system, this may come in the form of my human resources department—either filing a formal complaint, or learning about mental health resources available to our local network.

## Outside of My School and District, Who Else Can I Turn to for Support?

Burnout is real.

Witnessing injustices against our students and our families is excruciating. Experiencing injustices against ourselves or our colleagues is deeply painful. This work can be truly traumatizing.

Being connected to an external (outside of school) network is critical to ensure that we are tending to our mental health. As always, we must protect the identities of those we serve by never sharing personal details or other identifying information about those we serve or those we serve alongside.

This may come in the form of your house of faith, a charity network you belong to, old friends, family members, your bowling league, a domino group, a book club, or your knitting circle. Support could come in many forms.

Sometimes we know exactly what we might need (a happy hour with a friend, canceled plans, a day off, prayers, a fun distraction, a crying session, a pep talk, etc.). Being able to clearly communicate when you do know what you need can be a powerful way to get direct support. This may sound something like, "I'm at full capacity right now and I can really use tonight to be still and gather my thoughts. Let's reschedule. I'll reach out in the next few days."

Other days we might not know what we need, and that's okay, too. If you're able to identify the things you don't need, that's good to recognize and share with your circle. That might sound something like, "I'm not sure what I need, but right now I don't want someone to try to fix this or offer me solutions."

## How Do I Know When I Need to Take My Advocacy to the Next Level?

There may be times where you have to take your advocacy up a notch. A part of being equipped is knowing the laws that protect our students and families, and informing our colleagues and leadership if we believe that we are in violation of those laws.

When our states do local audits of schools or districts within the multilingual department (or other departments), sometimes we feel fearful that we're going to get "caught" doing something wrong. Friend, this audit is an opportunity for advocacy. Don't lie—in fact, sing like a canary! Tell it like it is! You might feel pressure from leadership to put on a nice show so that it looks like we have everything all set, but if that's not the case, tell the auditor. This is a chance for leadership to become more aware, and for our system to be better for those we serve.

Seeking out support of your local teachers' union is one avenue to get advocacy support. Your local union is a great place to start, but you can also receive support from your regional, state, or national unions.

There may be times where you have to file a formal complaint with your state's board of education about your school district's illegal practices. On most state websites, there is a formal process to do this, and it is often listed in detail on the website. Familiarize yourself with your local process in the event that you might need it.

You might also need to file a formal complaint against a school district or other body with the United States Department of Justice Civil Rights Division. The website also boasts seven different translations of the platform. It's important to know about the process in the event that you might need it.

It's good practice for us to explore these resources during moments where we don't feel like we are completely tapped out. Exploring these avenues during seasons of calm or when things are going just fine can really help us in the event that we'd ever need to go there in the future. It is important to equip ourselves by getting familiar with various avenues of additional advocacy support.

## How Do I Not Lose Myself in This Work?

At the end of the day, I'm a human being. I have loved ones. I have family and friends. I have an identity outside of my job.

I have interests that people would call "fluffy" or "silly," which is actually pretty disrespectful, especially if these are just things that bring me joy, and so to reduce them to being frivolous is quite rude, and even more—it's actually pretty dehumanizing. My "frivolous" interests are still worthy and deserving of time and attention and care and enjoyment.

## Scales, Spectrums, and Pulse Points

What's great about being a human being is that we grow. What's also important to note is that not all growth is linear. This work, in particular, is super-duper non-linear. We may find ourselves at different places in different continuums at different moments in life. Sometimes it may depend on our own positionality in a specific scenario. That's okay. We might have to continuously push ourselves when we're uncomfortable.

It is important to acknowledge our actions, beliefs, and changes we might need to enact. This can be painful. We might have to confront years of missing the mark. We might feel tremendous guilt or shame. However, it's not useful or helpful to shame ourselves. What matters next is how we move forward. How are we honest with ourselves? What have we learned that we can now carry forward into the future?

There may be seasons where we have to do more listening and learning but we cannot abdicate the opportunity to grow. We cannot opt out of the work.

Let's review all the elements we've explored throughout this journey.

In Chapter 1, we explored the big ideas of Equity and Advocacy and were introduced to the framework of Question, Equip, and Act.

In Chapter 2, we confronted dangerous rhetoric and mindsets that exist in our systems. We explored how to cultivate a healthy multilingual mindset that positions our multilingual learners as individuals who have tremendous value—not because of their language skills but because they are human beings.

In Chapter 3, we discussed linguistic identity and how this can shape our interactions and sense of belonging in our schools and systems. We confronted our own linguistic journeys, linguistic biases, and linguistic familiarity.

In Chapter 4, we identified problematic practices that begin at tier 1 for multilingual learners, including curricular resources and the constant message to "tweak" materials for multilingual learners as an afterthought. We explored strong practices for instruction across content areas at tier 1 for newcomer students and students at higher proficiency levels.

In Chapter 5, we identified multi-tiered systems of support structures that can result in either the over-identifying or under-identifying of multilingual learners in tiered services. We explored ways to make our systems more linguistically appropriate and responsive.

In Chapter 6, we explored gate-keeping of advanced, gifted, and enrichment programming. We identified various structures and protocols that provide more access to programs and also monitor the experience of multilingual learners participating in those programs.

In Chapter 7, we explored oppressive family engagement practices that exclude the families of multilingual learners. We unpacked language access, explored communication preferences, and ways for educators and leaders to focus on the experience of family engagement holistically.

Umm, what?! We've been busy.

Thank you, thank you, thank you for committing to this work. I appreciate the internal and external work you've done for those you serve. I see those hardships and the red flags. I know you've wrung your hands in defeat. I noticed those wins, celebrations and those green flags, too! I know that your work is making an impact in your system. Please, keep going. And please, be good to yourself. Thank you for being an advocate for equity for multilingual learners and families.

## Let's Go

As you continue to lean into your advocacy efforts, be encouraged. The more we continue to question ourselves and our systems, the more we can start to initiate conversations. The better equipped we become as individuals and collectively, the more equitable our decision making and action steps can become. The more we act, both individually and at the systems level, the more we can advocate for the multilingual learners and families that we serve.

Continue to question, equip, and act well beyond the pages of this book. Invite others into this work via entry points, but don't stop there! Seek out support, guidance, encouragement, and inspiration from the network around you. Together, we can Ignite Real Change! Let's go!

# References

Correa, M., Clester, S., & Arredondo, B. (2022). *Spanish is my superpower!* Random House.

Hammond, Z. L. (2015). *Culturally responsive teaching and the brain.* Corwin Press.

For Product Safety Concerns and Information please contact our EU
representative  GPSR@taylorandfrancis.com
Taylor & Francis Verlag GmbH, Kaufingerstraße 24, 80331 München, Germany

www.ingramcontent.com/pod-product-compliance
Lightning Source LLC
Chambersburg PA
CBHW070805230426
43665CB00017B/2497